Sword Techniques of MUSASHI and the Other Samurai Masters

Sword Techniques of MUSASHI and the Other Samurai Masters

Fumon Tanaka

Kodansha USA

The names of modern and contemporary Japanese appear in the Western order, while those of historical figures (pre-1868) are written in the traditional order: surname preceding given name.

For reference, the following chart shows those periods of Japanese history that will be most relevant to the discussion.

PERIOD NAME	APPROXIMATE DATES (A.D.)
Nara	710–784
Heian	794–1192
Kamakura	1192–1333
Muromachi	1336–1573
Nanbokucho	1336–1392
Sengoku	1467–1568
Azuchi-Momoyama	1573–1600
Edo	1600–1868
Meiji	1868–1912
Taisho	1912–1926
Showa	1926–1989
Heisei	1989–

(Historians do not agree on exactly when the various periods started and ended, so the dates listed are approximate. Japanese writing often refers as well to nengo, or shorter periods named after each reigning emperor. Some of these will be introduced where relevant.)

Originally published in Japanese as Zusetsu Miyamoto Musashi to Kengotachi no Kenpo by Kodansha, Tokyo, 2011.

Edited in cooperation with Musashi Editorial Ltd., and Matt Cotterill.
Designed by Point & Line Co., Ltd.

Published by Kodansha USA, Inc.
451 Park Avenue South
New York, NY 10016

Distributed in the United Kingdom and continental Europe by Kodansha Europe Ltd.

Printed in China.
ISBN 978-1-56836-475-9

First edition, 2013

www.kodanshausa.com

Library of Congress Cataloging-in-Publication Data

Tanaka, Fumon.
[Zusetsu miyamoto musashi to kengotachi no kenpo English]
Sword techniques of Musashi and other samurai masters / Fumon Tanaka.
pages cm
"Originally published in Japanese as Zusetsu Miyamoto Musashi to Kengotachi no Kenpo by Kodansha, Tokyo, 2011."
ISBN 978-1-56836-475-9
1. Miyamoto, Musashi, 1584-1645. 2. Martial artists—Japan—Biography. 3. Swordsmen—Japan—Biography. 4. Samurai—Japan—Biography. I. Title.
GV1141.72.M59T3613 2013
796.8092—dc23
[B]
2013003911

CONTENTS

CHAPTER 2 Rivals of Musashi 65

CHAPTER 3 World of Traditional Bujutsu 107

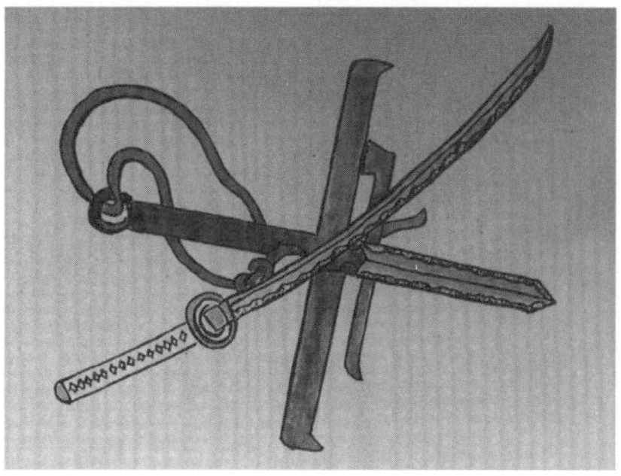

PROLOGUE

A "KEN" OR "TSURUGI" AND A "KATANA"

The history of Japan, which spans some 12,000~8,000 years, is also the history of swords. Martial arts have their roots firmly placed in the discipline of swordsmanship. In Japan, martial arts are regarded highly, and originated from a training that sought lethal methods of destroying or eliminating strong enemies. Budo training is rigorous and demanding, often pushing its devotees to the limits of their abilities. Practitioners train themselves in order to gain self-confidence and to survive no matter how tough the situation is, with originality and ingenuity.

This book offers an introduction to the ancient history of swords,* and this history is replete with many heroes and legends. According to Japan's oldest history book, the *Kojiki* ("Record of Ancient Matters"), in the mythological age, the deity known as Susanoo-no-Mikoto, wielding a ken in his hand, slew the fearsome monster named Yamata-no-Orochi (a gigantic, eight-headed serpent), to save a beautiful lady whose sisters had been devoured by the beast. After chopping off its eight heads, he discovered a ken named Ame-no-murakumo-no-tsurugi (the Sword of Gathering Clouds) inside the tail of the monster. This epic battle has led him to be regarded as the root of all Japanese swordsmanship.

The first Japanese Emperor, Jimmu, setting out from the island of Kyushu in southern Japan to explore the Mainland, waged savage battles against the indigenous forces at Osaka Bay. Fortune, however, was initially not in favor of Jimmu, and he suffered huge casualties to his forces. The blood of the war dead turned the color of the sea surface to crimson red. The fate of the great man began to change when he was given a divine ken by heavenly deities. With the sacred power of the ken named Futsu-no-mitama-no-tsurugi (Spiritual Sword), he later won many battles and ascended to the Imperial throne.

Generations later, Yamato Takeru-no-Mikoto, a son of the 12th Emperor Keiko, would come to inherit the legendary sword Ame-no-murakumo-no-tsurugi, handed down to him from his distant ancestor Susanoo-no-Mikoto. Takeru was a top military aristocrat, and was known for having wisdom, courage, and good fighting skills. Under an imperial order issued by his father, he travelled to Kyushu in order to vanquish the Kumaso tribe. He knew the leader of the group was

***Translator's note:** a "ken," or "tsurugi," is a straight sword with two edges, and a "katana" is a curved sword with a single edge. "Katana" is a descendent of the "ken."

Susanoo-no-Mikoto

Emperor Jimmu

Yamato Takeru-no-Mikoto

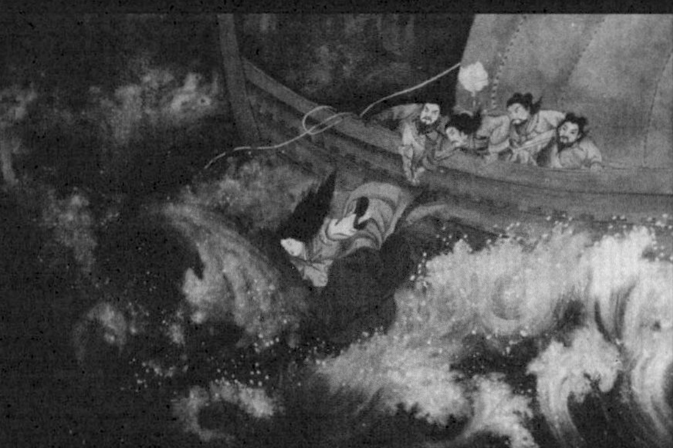

Princess Ototachibana—It is told that one day in the 4th century, a prince called Yamato Takeru-no-Mikoto was sailing his boat. Suddenly the sea became rough and there was a danger that his ship would sink. Yamato Takeru-no-Mikoto's wife, Princess Ototachibana, sacrificed herself as an offering to the gods by throwing herself into the sea, thus calming the tempestuous waves.

Jingu Kogo—Around the 2nd and the 3rd century, the Emperor Chuai, the second son of Yamato Takeru-no-Mikoto, had a wife named Empress Jingu, who went to Kyusyu to battle against the Kumaso tribe, using a sword similar to the tsurugi. She won the fight, and crossed the sea to fight more battles in Shiragi in old Korea. She was an outstanding warrior. She commanded the army and administrated the country's politics for decades.

very strong, so he approached him in disguise as a beautiful girl, and stabbed him to death. After the war, he explored eastern Japan, where he was deceived by a local warlord. He was lured into a grass field, and the tribe used fire arrows to ignite a blaze around him. Surrounded by the fierce inferno, he drew Ame-no-murakumo-no-tsurugi, and, using the power of wind infused in the sword, swept the grass around him. The fire was blown away and he survived. He would go on to conquer many tribes with this sword.

Against these historical backdrops, the unique martial arts that fused deities and humans together naturally formed to become the essence of Japan's spiritual culture. The three heroes above were worshipped as deities. Warlords won battles by praying to these deities. The ken became the symbol of divine power itself. Since then, ken have been regarded as the very soul of ancient warriors. In the same way, during the medieval age, katana, the descendent of ken, were taken as the soul of the samurai.

Swordsmanship, which evolved from the deep psyche of Japanese people over thousands of years, has an array of special meanings in Japan. The instant a practitioner begins his martial arts training, he gets an idea of the sublime world of deities. He believes in gods, and seeks out the existence of deities. As a trainee of musha-shugyo (Budo training), he travels in the other world, both spiritually and physically, domestically and abroad, and immerses himself in extreme training. In the religious field he achieves enlightenment with the help of deities. In the field of technique he invents his original, consummate skills by listening to the voices of deities. And in the field of arts and crafts he creates his works as a mission from gods. He offers endless thanks to deities for his innate talents that have been fostered and have now thrived.

In Japanese traditional martial arts, a practitioner learns skills to kill and destroy all of his enemies, and at the same time he sets on a journey to ascertain psychical phases. At the advanced stages of technical skills, his mentality endures internal conflicts between ambivalence and enlightenment, good and evil. Thus, he must also train academically to explore profound philosophy. In due time, he reaches the knowledge of deep psyche; he quests for invincible Budo skills and a peaceful mind. Once he achieves this state—nirvana-like, invincible, and ideal—he is led to the ultimate honor and harmony of controlling his opponents without killing or hurting them.

"Invincible" has two meanings. One is that a Budo practitioner is too strong to

The Taika Reforms—In 672 the Emperor Tenmu killed the head of the resistance Sogano Iruka, with Moroha-no-tsurugi. This event had a profound influence on history.

Kibasen (cavalry battles)—In the 12th century the tsurugi attained a status as the very soul of royalty, and ceased to be used in battle. The period of the katana-wielding warrior took its place, and it was around this time that horse-back sword techniques were developed.

Genko (Mongol invasion against Japan)—The Yuan Dynasty (Mongol-led China) attempted to conquer Japan twice in 1274 and 1281, but the invasions were repelled by Japanese warriors using katana and the strength of the gods. Some 200,000 Gen soldiers lost their lives. ("Yuan" in Chinese is pronounced "Gen" in Japanese)

Nitta Yoshisada—A story goes that at the end of the Kamakura Period (1334) a famous commander named Nitta Yoshisada gave the gods an offering of a golden sword by throwing it into the sea. In so doing he gained the support of the sea gods who pulled in the tide, thus allowing his army to sail faster and defeat their enemies, the Kamakura shogunate army.

The Incident out of the Sakurada Gate—Ii Naosuke was a powerful figure in the Tokugawa Government. He was infamous for oppressing and executing many scholars and philosophers. He was killed in a surprise attack by a group of eighteen warriors in front of the Sakurada gate of Edo Castle.

Shogitai—At the end of the Warrior period (1868), the Tokugawa Shogunate organized 2,000 of its vassals to an army called Shogitai. Fighting with the new, modern-equipped Meiji Government soldiers, they nevertheless shunned the use of guns and cannons in favor of swords.

be challenged. The other is that he has developed his mentality to become so refined that no one wants to fight him anymore. Both states are the results of a profound understanding of pacifism as god's will. The original thoughts of Japanese Bushido evolved into the ultimate state of muto (no-sword), where one no longer needs to rely on swords.

FEATURES OF KENJUTSU TRAINING

Kenjutsu employs lethal techniques for battle. No matter how highly a practitioner refines his skills, or how extensively he uses his techniques, it is of little importance. The true purpose of kenjutsu is to embark on a quest in which the mind can control physical techniques. Samurai put emphasis on the power of the mind rather than physical techniques, and considered the mind to be essential in controlling duels.

The essence of techniques is kata, and each school practices varying disciplines of kata. Kata are formalized techniques, rendered as body movements. It is the mind, however, that makes effective use of skills, and this concept is very profound. Initially, when a warrior faces his enemies, he feels that he wants to defeat them. But this is only a manifestation of passion; it is not his real thought. Deep within himself, he fears fighting against strong enemies, or he feels the urge to escape. Overcoming this weakness of the mind is the fundamental purpose of his training as a samurai. He continues his training, and over time he forms a strong and firm will, and understands theoretical aspects of fights.

Understanding how the mind works and employing the use of the body are two separate issues. So, by refining good kata, the warrior gains insight into his true psyche. This is the essence of kenjutsu. Thus with true mind and true techniques, a warrior is able to defeat his opponents each time he fights. This elevated state has been attained by many swordsmen, such as Miyamoto Musashi and Tsukahara Bokuden, among many others. When one reaches this state, one has no reason to fight anymore. This training method is derived from the original Bushido culture of Japan, and is a state that competitive sports employing only body movement can never achieve. For these reasons, traditional swordsmanship is still being transmitted through generations even today.

The Seinan War—1877. This was the last war in Japan in which katana were used. The rise of the new Meiji Government had angered the traditional samurai class, who waged many armed uprisings against the government. These uprisings were characterized more by ambushes employing hand-to-hand combat with swords as opposed to modern weapons such as guns and cannons. The war claimed many lives.

A picture of a standard government soldier being attacked by the rebellion army.

Charging forward without fearing the bullets, attacking the enemy.

A surprise attack.

Even when wounded, soldiers could use the sword as a walking stick to stand up.

Fighting until the last man standing.

An advancing female warrior.

The women fought with naginatas.

Spies, even women, were tied up and cut down.

BLACK AND WHITE COSTUMES IN JAPAN

Black—the color of costumes of traveling Buddhist monks

The colors of formal attire are designated black or white according to rituals from the old days in Japan. In today's Japan, a formal costume is composed of a kimono and a haori jacket in black. Such clothing is said to follow the example of the black attire of "unsui," traveling monks in the Zen sect of Buddhism.

Kimonos developed from the everyday clothes of ordinary people in the Muromachi period (1336-1573). Haori jackets were originally the cloaks worn by spiritual masters in Taoism, seeking to get help from deities or hermits. Both Zen monks and Taoist masters trained themselves by traveling all over the country. The fashion development demonstrates a characteristic of Japanese people—the ability to improve.

White—the color of costumes of gods

White has been the color of gods since "kamiyo"—the Age of Deities. For example, Sumiyoshi Taisha Shrine in Osaka Prefecture holds a Shinto ritual of rice planting every year. In the shrine ceremony, miko (maidens serving the gods) powder their faces in white and become possessed by a "ryujin"—the god of water—and they dedicate a dance to the god praying for rain. The tradition is based on the belief that gods prefer white. By the same token, Shinto priests wear white.

Japanese martial arts originated from prayers to gods in ancient Shinto religion. Thus when samurai carried out harakiri suicide, they were dressed completely in white, from their undergarments to outer clothing. Even today, Japanese people wear white in their coffins, following a tradition that holds we need to be united with gods in white costumes when we cross over to the netherworld.

Based on the national conventional mind, in real martial arts—as opposed to sports or calisthenics for mere recreation—wearing white "dogi" (training clothes) and white hakama together is the sign of one's strong mindset in a burial outfit. The attire is designed to show that one realizes that he or she is prepared to die at any time and therefore can cope with anything.

In battlefields or real combat, Japanese people believe deeply that they have to overwhelm death and leave it up to gods whether they live or die. That is part of the Japanese psyche. Accordingly, in classical martial arts, devoting ourselves to god, we are to study the matters of life or death by practicing rigorous katas. The traditional Bujutsu espouses a world in which we learn the view of life and death.

Unsui (wandering monk)
A priest undertaking an ascetic journey or practicing mendicancy is called an "unsui" (an itinerant priest). These black-colored clothes became the formal wear of such priests. They were called "Seiso no monpuku" (formal wear.)

Kuro montsuki (formal wear)
A black outfit called kuro montsuki. Holding a fan is part of the warrior's etiquette.

Kuro montsuki (monpuku)
When a warrior dresses with the Kuro montsuki (monpuku) inside a room, the etiquette dictates holding a sword in one's hand.

Shiro shozoku (white clothing)
When committing seppuku (harakiri), worshipping gods before one commits to the ritual, it is customary to wear pure white clothes, in order to be recognized by gods.

Shiro muku (white kimono for the wedding ceremony)
Since ancient times, weddings have been considered one of the biggest events in a person's life, therefore in order to be blessed by gods, it is common etiquette to wear pure white clothes, and to make the wedding vows in front of gods.

Kyutei Kojo (the Imperial princess)
As descendants of the sun goddess Amaterasu-omi-kami, the women of the imperial family used to work in the Shinto temples as shrine maidens, also known as "miko" or "saiodai." They were the representatives of the gods. These women used to paint their faces, necks, and hands in white, the color favored by the gods. Even in modern times white makeup is used during Shinto ceremonies.

Maiko (apprentice geisha)
The origin of the white makeup worn by maikos and geishas came originally from the "miko" who used to wear white makeup when working for gods in ceremonies.
This is a tradition which remains even today.

CHAPTER 1

The Real Miyamoto Musashi

THE TRUTH ABOUT MIYAMOTO MUSASHI

In the history of Japanese kenjutsu, the name Miyamoto Musashi is legendary, and he is revered as a sword god. The real Miyamoto Musashi lived about 450 years ago, at the end of the Warring States Period. He was born in 1584, although historians differ as to the location of his birth. Musashi was raised in violent times; it was the end of the Warring States Period, a turbulent chapter in Japanese history of social upheaval and military conflict. By the time he reached manhood, however, Japan had become a warless, peaceful society, Bushido was progressing towards establishment, and attitudes towards social values were fundamentally changing. Musashi adapted to the changing of the times, and lived a heroic life that combined the sword and the pen; a life that has kept his name legendary until this day.

Musashi studied kenjutsu in his early childhood in order to become an unbeatable warrior. At the age of thirteen he duelled Arima Kihe from the Shinto-ryu and won, and at the age of sixteen he duelled a warrior named Akiyama in Tajima (today Hyogo prefecture), again defeating his opponent. By the time he was thirty Musashi was unbeaten in no fewer than sixty-six duels. He was a truly gifted swordsman. In those days warriors who were duelling other ryuhas (schools) had to be extremely strong, talented, and experienced in battle. Indeed, the path to success and fortune for many warriors lay in raising one's name as a master swordsman and building one's reputation through victory in duels.

Times began to change when Musashi was in his thirties. Japan settled into a period of peace, and the role of the warrior class began to change, with many becoming government workers. Aside from the deep training of the kenjutsu techniques, a spiritual dimension to the martial arts began to flourish, and warriors were starting to explore deep psychological and philosophical sides of the sword arts. Adjusting to the winds of the times, Musashi stopped duelling and started researching the inner secrets and theories of the kenjutsu techniques, in order to seek the deeper truths of their existence. He also started to make tsuba

A colored woodblock print of Miyamoto Musashi in *Bugei Hyakunin Isshu*.

The stone monument to console Miyamoto Musashi's soul.

for swords and small swords to be used as shuriken. In addition, Musashi embarked on many cultural activities—he became a first-class painter and wrote Zen-related renga poems, heightening the level of his cultural knowledge. At the same time he continued his research of kenjutsu and combat tactics as a basic means to understanding the path of life. These activities characterized much of Musashi's life.

Musashi's full name was Miyamoto Musashi no kami Fujiwara Harunobu. The renowned school of Miyamoto Haronobu's kenpo, Enmei-ryu, which uses both swords at the same time, was originally founded by Miyamoto Harunobu's ancestor, Miyamoto Musashi no kami Yoshimoto. Yoshimoto studied from the highly renowned priest, Enmei-ajari, secret techniques of Bujutsu and the essence of Buddhist philosophy, which were the inner secrets of Enmei-ajari's ryuha. Thus when he founded his own ryuha he named it Enmei-ryu as a tribute to his teacher Enmei-ajari. Enmei-ajari was the younger brother of Asai Nagamasa, the daimiyo (feudal ruler) of Omihokutobu (Shiga prefecture), but Enmei-ajari decided to leave the military life and choose the path of priesthood.

Shrike on a dead tree drawn by Musashi.

Dynamic handwriting of *ryu* (dragon) by Miyamoto Musashi.

Picture of a wild goose drawn by Miyamoto Musashi.

Portrait of Miyamoto Musashi.

ENMEI JITTE-RYU

Miyamoto Musashi was a master of the two-sword techniques using the daito and the shoto in both hands, something that led to the popular belief that he was the inventor of this fighting method. This is in fact not true. There are old written scrolls that prove the original two-sword fighting techniques come from Enmei-ryu. These scrolls were published in the author's earlier book *Samurai Fighting Arts* (Kodansha International 2003).

The uncle of Musashi, Aoki Jouemon, was the successor of the Enmei-ryu, and his grandson, Aoki Tetsujin, also succeeded this ryuha, which is referred to by many names, including: Enmei jitte-ryu, Tetsujin jitte-ryu, Tetsujin Enmei-ryu, and Enmei Itto-ryu. Despite the numerous names, the techniques are all the same. The main feature of the Enmei-ryu is a special folding weapon called a karakuri jitte. The blade is shaped like a spear blade so it is also called yari jitte. When not used for fighting it can be folded and placed inside the belt or the inner part of the kimono. It is a secret, hidden weapon. In addition, when fighting with the two-sword technique, the daito is held in the right hand, while the jitte can be used in place of the shoto in the left hand.

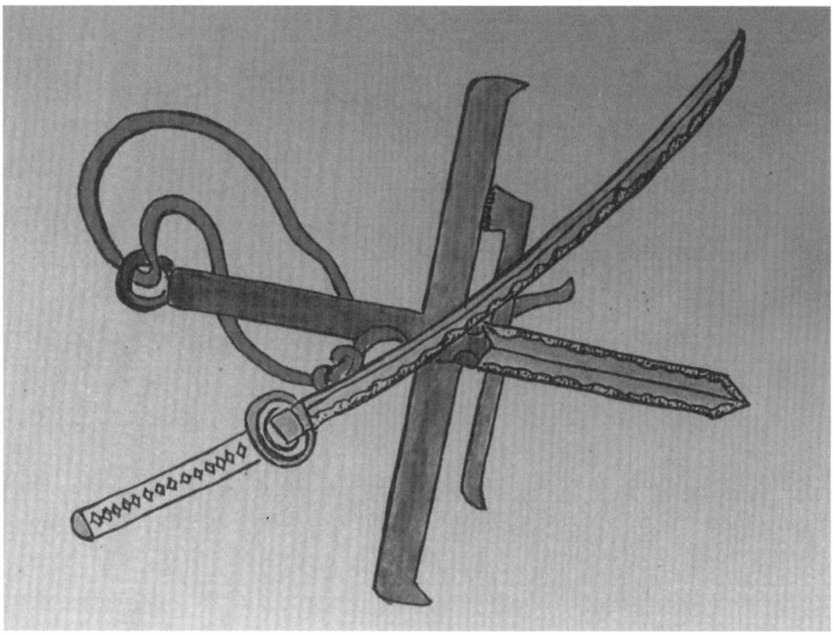

17th-Century scrolls of the Tetsujin jitte-ryu that show drawings of the jitte.

How to hold a jitte in one's hand.

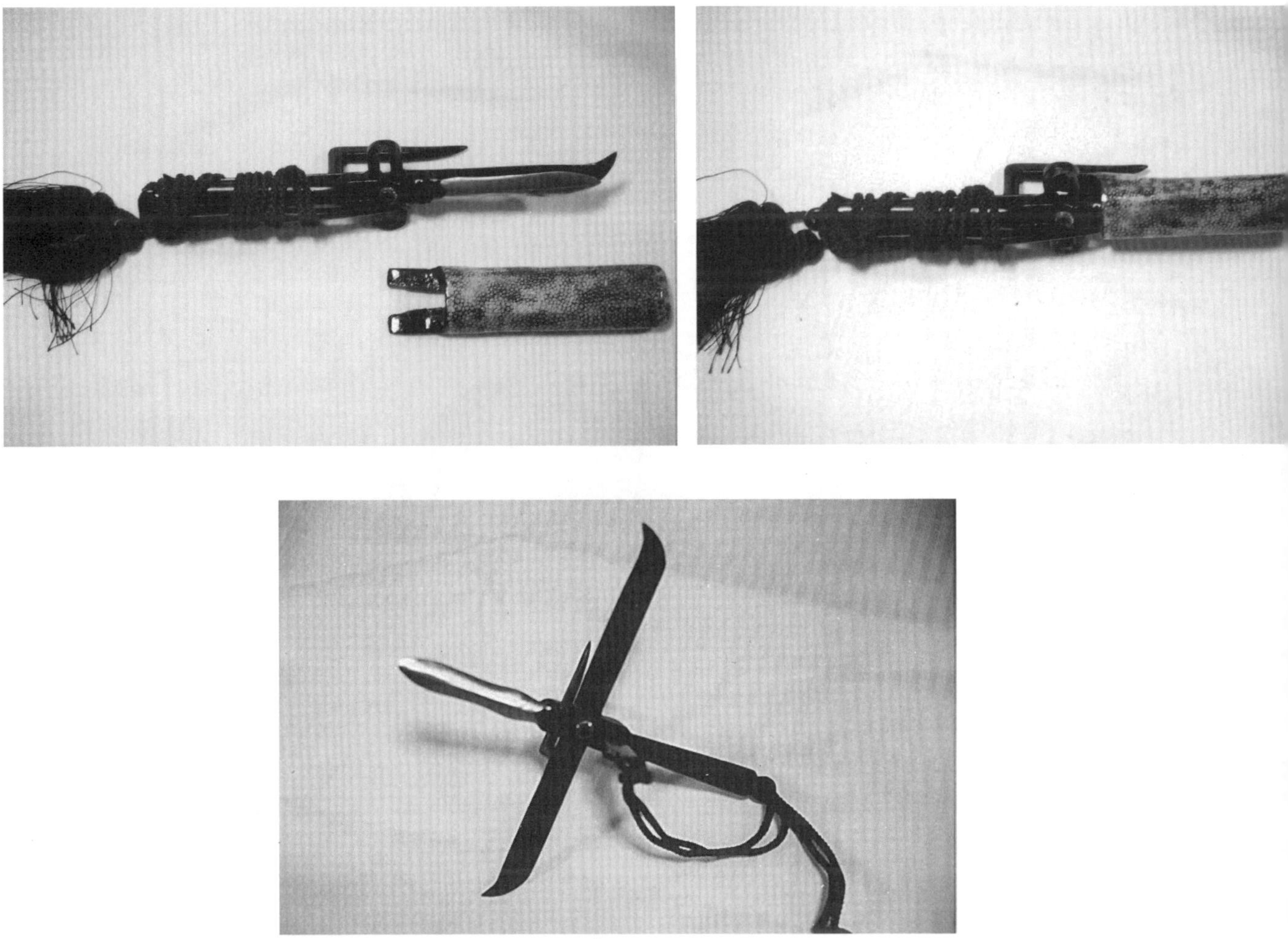

How to assemble a jitte from its folded form.

The original form of the jitte comes from Jumonji-yari, adjusting to the enemy's weapon or the range of fight. It is also possible to attach a handle to this weapon, making it very functional. The inventor of this weapon was the founder of Enmei-ryu, the ancestor of Musashi, Miyamoto Musashi no kami Yoshimoto. It is said that Yoshimoto was a ninja under the service of Toyotomi Hideyoshi, and that his character was very mysterious. Yoshimoto indeed invented the jitte, but this was against the background of the fact that the most effective and practical weapon on the battlefield was the long-handled spear. As a ninja he had a concept of a weapon that could be removed from the handle and used as a hidden weapon. To be able to carry the spear at all times was a great honor for a warrior. The Enmei-ryu merged the soul of the samurai and the sword with the jumonji spear, and created new techniques.

This tsuba was made by Musashi, and is known as "Musashi Tsuba."

Jittedori no kamae

1

2

3

4

5

6

7

8

The father of Musashi Munisai in the beginning taught the Enmei-ryu two-sword techniques, and then he founded the Muso-ryu and Tori-ryu.

MUSO-RYU

17th-Century Muso-ryu, Nitokenpo scrolls.

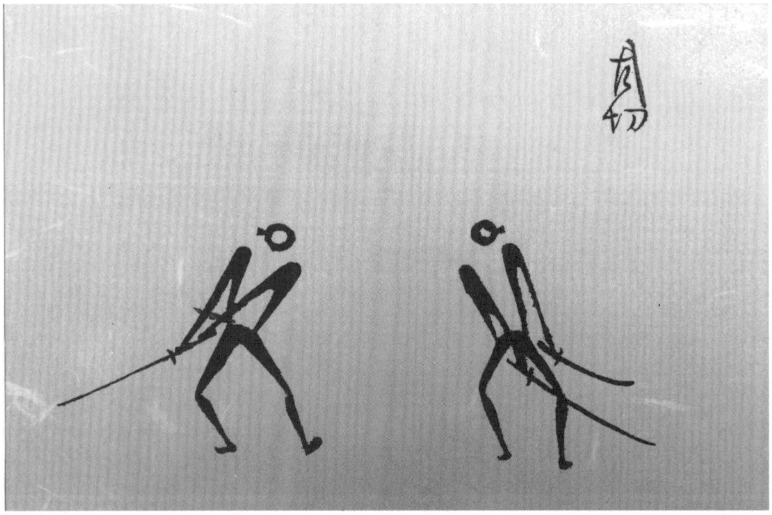

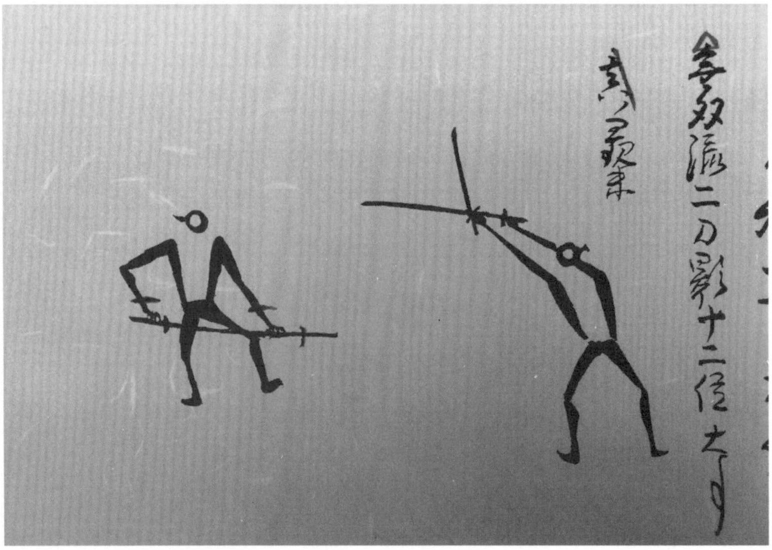

A hand scroll written by a disciple of Miyamoto Munisai.

TORI-RYU

Scrolls of Tori-ryu written by the adopted son of Munisai, Mizuta Muemon, in 1603. Muemon was also known as another Musashi.

When Mizuta Muemon became the adopted child of Munisai, he changed his name from Miyamoto Musashi no kami Masakatsu to Masatsugu.

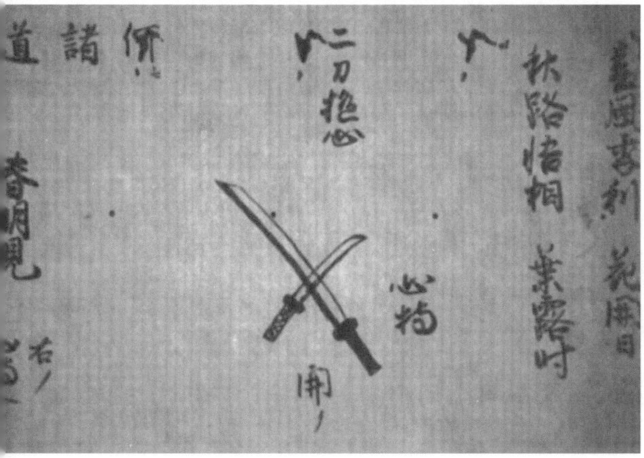

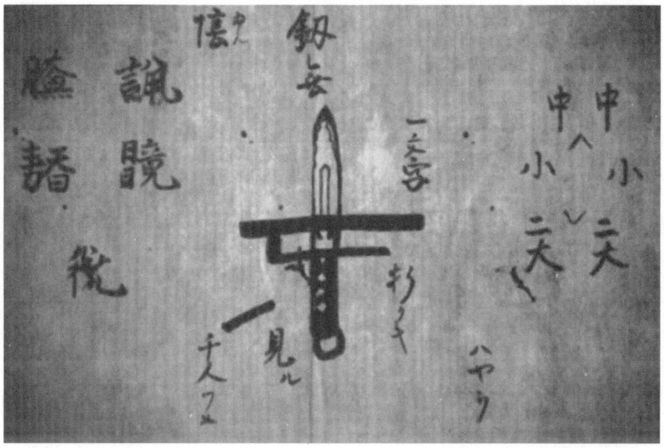

A hand scroll of Tori- ryu, made in the 17th century.

KYUSHIN-RYU

The cousin of Musashi or the son of the cousin Aoki kyushin Ienao, separated from the Enmei-ryu and founded the Kyushin-ryu.

These pictures show scrolls that were written in 1614. The Kyushin-ryu was part of the same group as the Tetsuji-Enmei-ryu, Muso-ryu, and the Tori-ryu. They all practiced two-sword techniques. In these pictures it is possible to see that the jitte that is depicted in the Tori-ryu scrolls has the same form as the Enmei-ryu jitte.

From observing the scrolls of the Muso-ryu, Tori-ryu, Tetsujin Enmei-ryu, and the Kyushin-ryu, it is possible to see that two-sword techniques were being practiced long before Musashi's time.

In his late years Musashi changed the name of Enmei-ryu to Nito ichi-ryu and then to Niten ichi-ryu. Niten (two skies) are said to be inspired by the sun and the moon.

In 1612, when Musashi was twenty-eight, he had a duel with Sasaki Kojiro on Funashima. (This duel and Kojiro's ryuha are discussed in Chapter 2.)

1

2

An emakimono (hand scroll with pictures) of Kyushin-ryu, made in the 17th century.

3

4

5

6

7

8

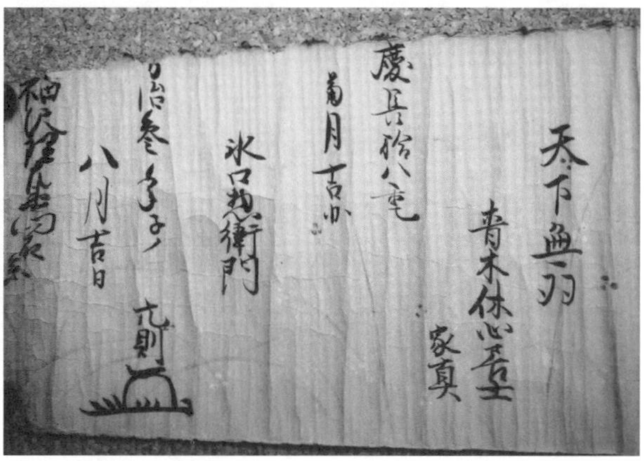
9

RE-ENACTMENT OF SASAKI KOJIRO'S SWORD DRAW

In Eiji Yoshikawa's novel *Musashi* (published by Kodansha International, 1981) it is described that Sasaki Kojiro had a special long sword that he used to carry on his back and draw it from there. This is a very advanced technique.

The author's daughter and his students, three female swordswomen, demonstrate this special draw.

Batto no kamae.

The beginning of the draw.

Separating the sword from the saya, then drawing it.

Immediately standing in gedan or katsugi kamae.

Hasso no kamae.

Ichimonji no kamae.

Gedan no kamae.

MUSASHI'S SECRET TECHNIQUE: TENGU TOBI

In the famous duel on Funashima, Musashi used the tengu tobi technique against Sasaki Kojiro's secret technique tsubame gaeshi, and defeated his opponent. In today's Niten ichi-ryu and other ryuha that are related to Musashi, however, I was unable to find any references to this technique. Therefore, the tengu tobi was recreated based on depictions in the novel *Musashi* and oral tradition.

1

2

3

4

The moment of impact of tengu tobi.

5

Technique Explanation

The party on the left, representing Musashi, is using an exact copy of the wooden sword that Musashi used in that duel. He stands in hasso no kamae. On the right side of the picture the party representing Sasaki Kojiro (using a sword that is 8cm longer than the one Kojiro used in the duel) is standing in hidari kuruma no kamae. She performs the first cut of tsubame gaeshi in order to cut Musashi's legs. Musashi executes the tengu tobi jump, dodging Kojiro's attack, and hits the top of Kojiro's head in the leap, winning the duel.

THE GARDENS DESIGNED BY MUSASHI

From the ages of thirty-four (1618) to forty-two (1626), Musashi served as the subject of the famous Ogasawara clan in Akashi (today Hyogo prefecture). But he did not serve as a warrior, rather as an administrator. He was in charge of planning the layout of the city area. Moreover, he drew up the blueprint for the gardens of the Akashi Castle and also those of many temples. As a strategist, Musashi planned the castle, the temple gardens, and the city layout for

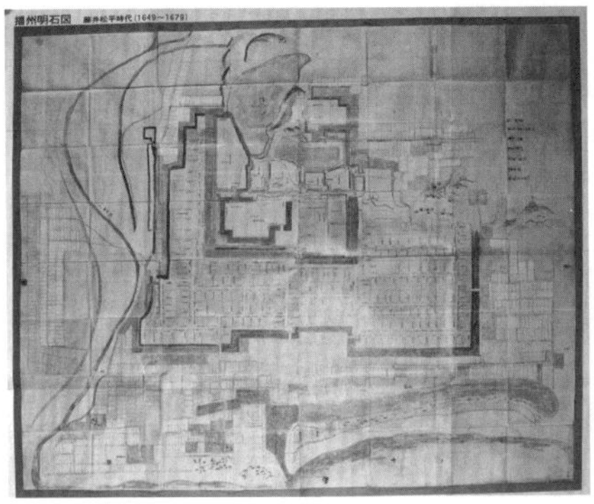

The urban planning of Akashi City.

The Akashi Castle.

The facade of Honshoji Temple.

The garden designed by Miyamoto Musashi in Honshoji Temple.

The facade of Zenrakuji Temple.

The garden designed by Miyamoto Musashi in Enman-in area, Zenrakuji Temple.

The Traditions of Gardens in Buddhist Temples

The rock garden in Ryuanji Temple, Kyoto.

The rock garden in Negoroji Temple, where legends of Ninjas still remain.

times of peace. While planning the city, however, he also kept in mind that a war might occur, so he planned the city taking into account such strategic factors.

The origin of Japanese gardens dates back to the Heian Period (794~1192) when aristocrats made their own gardens in their mansions under the influences of the elegant court culture of ancient China. Later, many Buddhist temples got to make their own gardens.

Temples, as halls of Buddhism, were places to enlighten and protect their followers, but in times of war they could also serve as forts or accommodations to station military units. High-profile warriors were therefore very familiar with the temple gardens.

MUSASHI'S SHURIKENJUTSU

In 1629 Musashi went back to his ronin (masterless warrior) way of life, and opened a kenjutsu dojo near Osaka and Kyoto. Then, in 1630, he went to Nagoya in Owari (Aichi prefecture), and stayed at the Yagyu clan residence where he taught the two-sword techniques of Enmei-ryu to Yagyu Hyogonosuke.

After Musashi left for the capital Edo, Yagyu Hyogonosuke developed top secret techniques against enemies who used two swords. These techniques are still being passed on today; they are explained in detail in Chapter 4.

From 1632 Musashi lived in Edo for three years, and adopted a child called Yoemon (also called Takemura Musashi), whom he taught kenjutsu and tokenjutsu (shurikenjutsu—knife-throwing techniques). The shurikenjutsu is known as the Takemura-ryu.

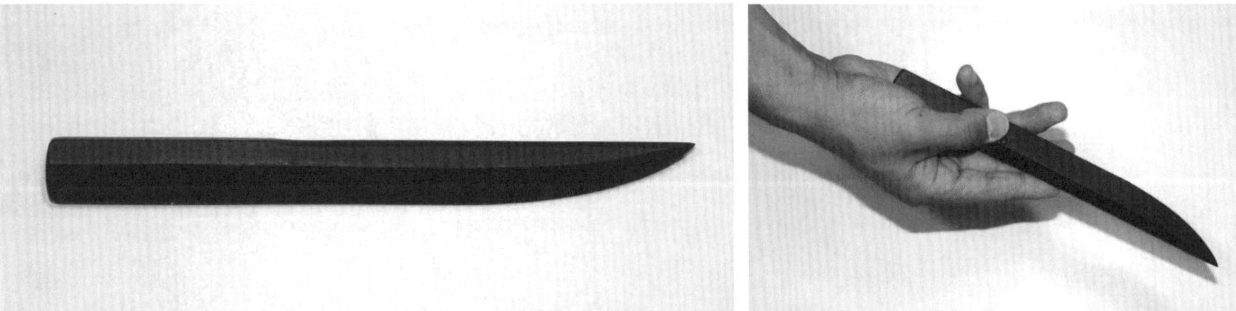

The shuriken contrived by Miyamoto Musashi.

A throwing form of a shuriken.

The statue of Amakusa Shiro Tokisada.

The Simabara Castle, which accommodated the armies of the Tokugawa government and other feudal lords, was also used as the combat operations center.

In 1635 Musashi went to Ogura in Kyushu, and stayed in the house of his adopted child Miyamoto Iori. In 1637 the oppressed followers of Christianity started an uprising against the government. The Christian rebels were barricaded in the Hara Castle in the Shimabara area. This uprising became known as the Shimabara Revolt. Musashi was about fifty-two years old at the time. As a result of this incident, Musashi's son Miyamoto Iori joined the Ogasawara clan as a commander. There is a story that Musashi, in order to support his son, also joined the battle. While climbing to the Hara Castle, large rocks were dropped on them, and one of the rocks seriously injured one of Musashi's legs.

The Tokugawa Shogunate soldiers had been stationed in the Shimabara Castle, and from there they commanded the attack. The Christian rebels were barracked in the Hara Castle, surrounded by the sea on three sides; a very good strategic place.

In 1640, when Musashi was fifty-six, he was invited by the lord of the Kumamoto Castle, Hosokawa Tadatoshi, to a salon that was made for top-class warriors. There he passed some days quietly relaxing and entertaining himself with renga writing. The secret writings of very important Niten ichi-ryu, kenjutsu, and strategy techniques; the *Hyoho sanjugokajo*, the *Jucchinoden*, and some others still remain.

In 1643, when Musashi was sixty, in a cave called Reigendo in the Iwaso mountain, he wrote *The Book of Five Rings* (Gorin-no-sho) and the *Dokkodo*. In 1644, when Musashi was sixty-one, he passed away.

The stone wall of Hara Castle. When Musashi climbed the wall, he was hit by a huge rock and was seriously injured.

Portrait of Amakusa Sihro Tokisada, the rebel leader.

The Hara Castle remains — a natural stronghold, in which the Christian rebels barricaded themselves.

THE REIGAN CAVE

It is believed that Miyamoto Musashi's soul dwells in the Reigan cave. Even these days many people visit the cave to worship. It is considered a holy place. One day, the author and the soke of Niten ichi-ryu, master Yonehara Kameo, went to the Reigan cave and conducted a demonstration of Miyamoto Musashi's single sword secret technique, the toraburi, as an offering to Miyamoto Musashi's soul.

The Kumamoto Castle.

Soke Yonehara and the author heading to the Reigan cave.

In front of the Reigan cave, talking about *The Book of Five Rings*, secret scrolls, and contemplating Musashi's legacy.

TORABURI NO KATA

Uchidachi–Soke Yonehara, Shitachi–Tanaka Fumon

First both parties stand in hasso. Then, the shitachi pulls back the right leg and hides the sword behind his body, Toraburi no kamae. From this position the enemy can't see the sword, so he attacks the inner part of the shoulders. The shitachi steps with the right leg to the right and slightly forward, and cuts the enemy's neck. End of technique.

THE BOOK OF FIVE RINGS WRITTEN BY MUSASHI

Musashi wrote several documents of his Niten ichi-ryu which have been passed down through the generations: *Gorin-no-sho* (*The Book of Five Rings*), *Jicchi-no-den* (*Transmission of Ten Pieces of Wisdom*), *Hyoho 35 Kajo* (*Thirty-five Pieces of Martial Arts*), *Dokkodo* (*The Lone Way*), among others. Here, I will introduce some of them.

First, Musashi wrote *Gorin-no-sho* in 1644. He wrote the secret scrolls in the Reigan cave. The Niten ichi-ryu kenjutsu was upgraded little by little through harsh training, and it finally reached the ultimate goal of the secrets of martial arts.

Musashi documented the process in the five scrolls: *chi* (earth), *sui* (water), *ka* (fire), *fuu* (wind), and *kuu* (air). He gave them to his disciple, Terao Magonojou.

The contents of the scrolls are introduced in detail in *The Book of Five Rings*. "Five rings" is a term of Buddhism which explains a basic human life, dividing a human body into five parts. When a person dies, people make a stupa by piling five stones, and pray for that person. It is known as a "gorin-no-to" (stupa of five rings). Buddhism teaches that a human body consists of the five elements: earth, water, fire, wind, and air.

Earth is the legs. Humans take crops from the earth, eat, digest, and return them to the earth.

Water is the belly. Water is indispensable to a human, and a part of the body which stores liquid is the belly, and is called "the water."

Fire is the chest. A human eats food and burns it inside the chest to maintain his body temperature.

Wind is the space from the throat to the mouth, because respiration resembles wind.

The head is called "air." A human is compared to a small cosmos. The head is the source of thoughts, inspiration, intellect, and of discerning good from evil.

The scroll of *The Book of Five Rings.*

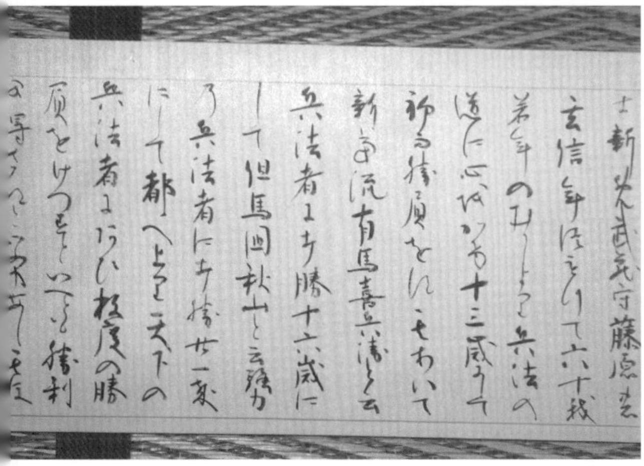

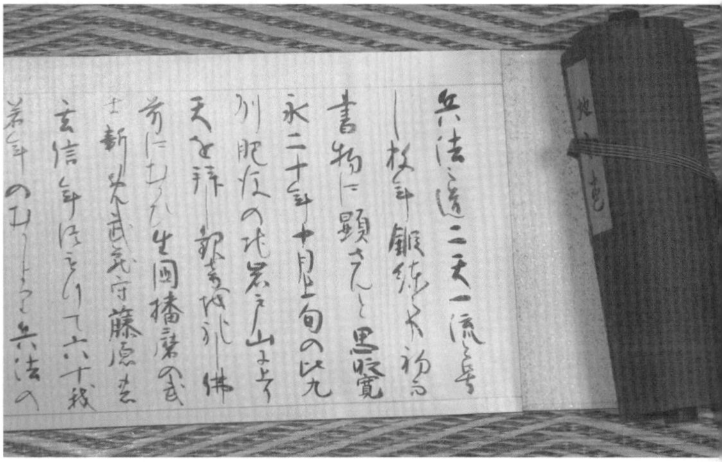

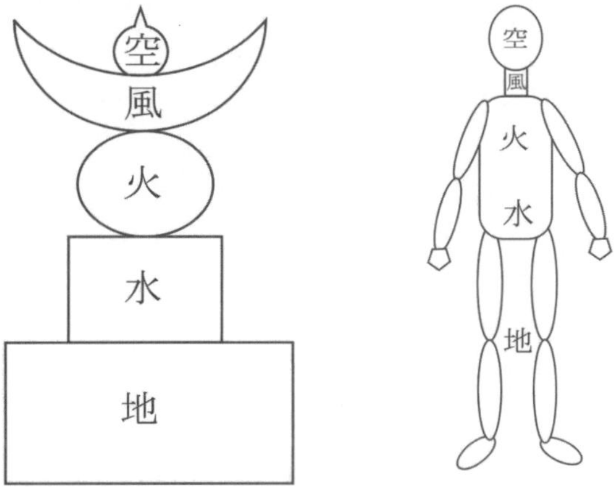

The chart of the five rings of a human body, and the stupa made of five stones.

DOKKODO WRITTEN BEFORE HIS DEATH

Miyamoto Musashi gave this scroll to Terao Magonojo on May the 12th 1645 shortly before his death. In the book, Musashi wrote some lectures on devoting one's whole life to upgrading martial arts skills, by leading one's life in a down-to-earth, independent, selfless, uncompromising way. The handwriting of this scroll is very similar to that of Musashi's, but it is uncertain if he was the true author.

The scroll of *Dokkodo*.

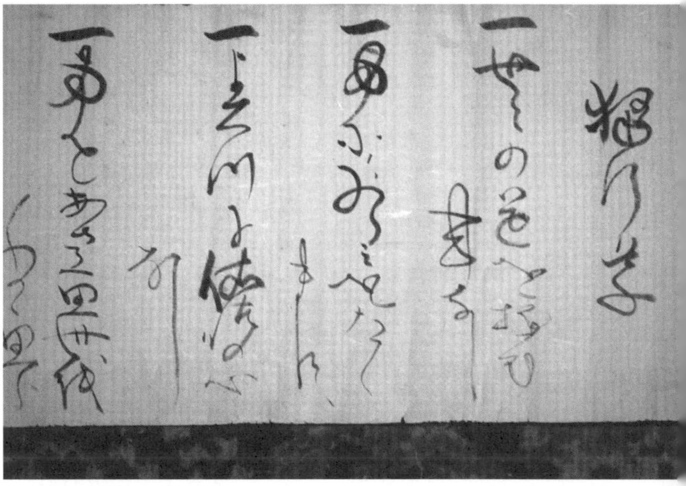

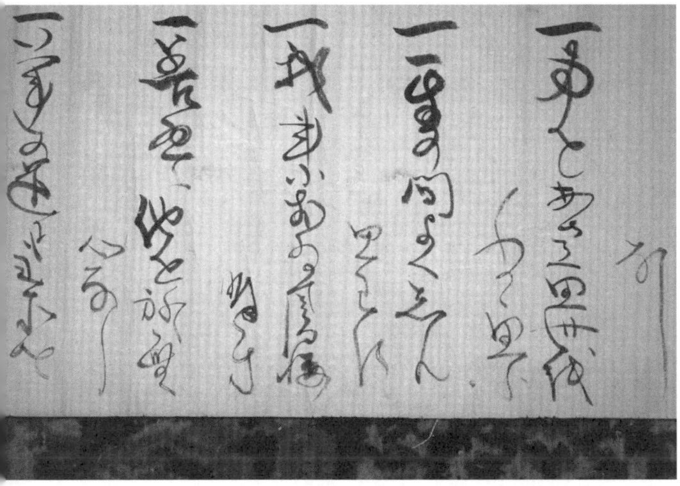

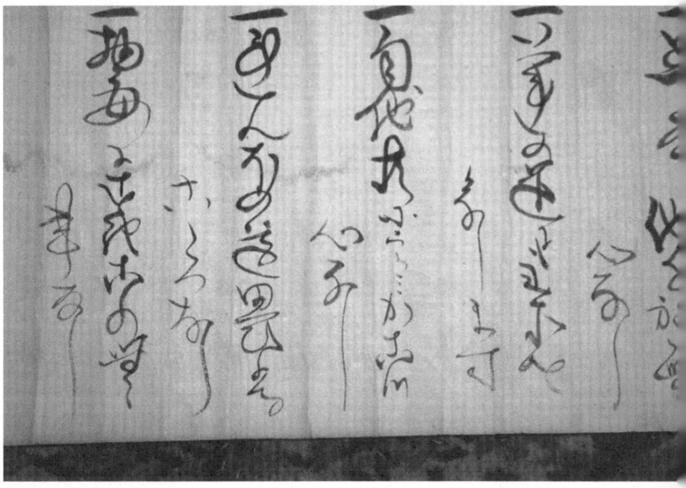

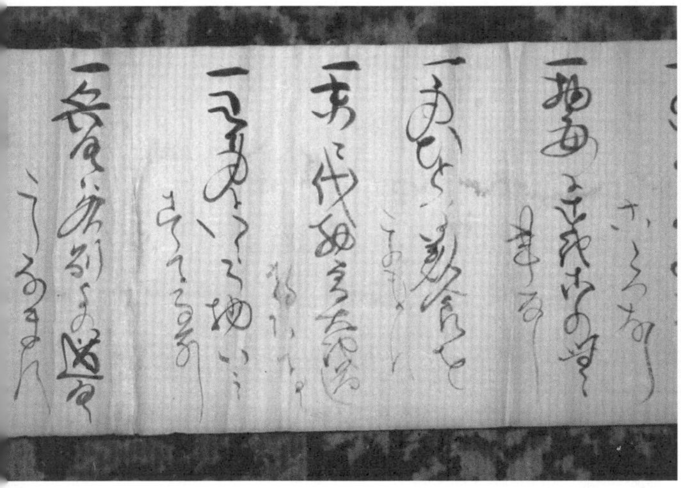

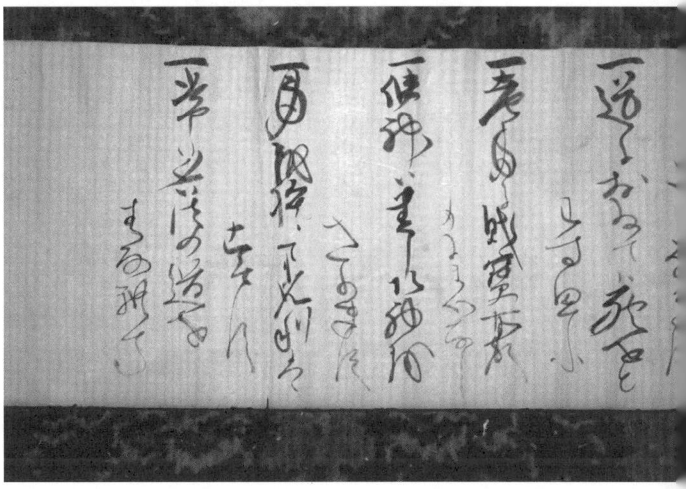

THE WEAPON CALLED A KAIKEN

This weapon is called a kaiken. Miyamoto Musashi used to hide it all the time in the inner side of his clothes, close to his chest. It is generally believed that Musashi had many enemies, from former duellists bearing a grudge to other warriors jealous of his status, and his life was in constant danger; he could have been killed at any moment. In case of a surprise attack this weapon was placed inside the kimono. Sleeping with the right arm holding the weapon inside the kimono also ensured that this hand, which is the stronger one for using the sword, would not be cut off.

The form of this weapon is more than 10,000 years old, dating back to the Stone Age, when it was used for farming and gathering vegetables. There is an authentic 6,000-year-old kaiken stored in an archive, but unfortunately it was not possible to publish its picture in this book. Therefore, I made a replica of a kaiken that was used in the warrior period made out of steel. Using this kaiken, a re-enactment of one of its techniques is shown here.

A kaiken
Musashi always carried one in his kimono for self-defence.

Kata no.1

1

2

3

4

5

6

Kata no.2

1

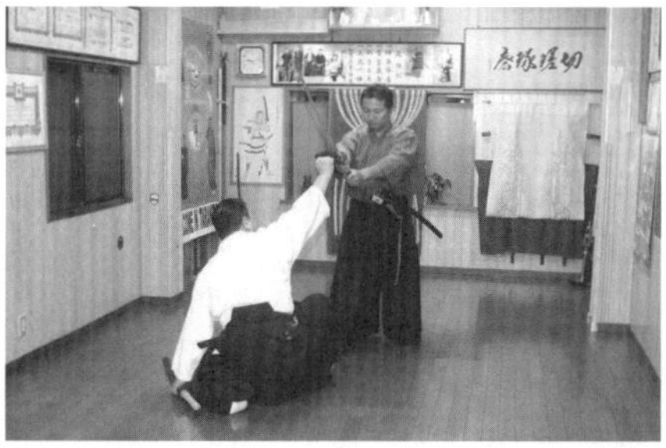
2

3

4

Technique Explanation

While sleeping, in order not to have the sword stolen, the warrior uses it as a pillow. Inside the clothes he holds the kaiken. With his right hand, the enemy comes from the side of the legs quietly. The astute warrior will notice the enemy approaching with the intention to kill, and will be waiting for the attack.

Kata no. 1

The enemy attacks from daijodan. The warrior blocks the attack with the kaiken and the sword slides to the right side. The warrior attacks the enemy with the kaiken straight to the face. End of technique.

Kata no. 2

The enemy attacks from daijodan. The warrior blocks the sword with the kaiken and at the same time holds the sword with his left hand and attacks the wrist of the enemy, taking it down. With the right hand holding the kaiken he attacks to the face. End of technique.

NITEN ICHI-RYU SWORD TECHNIQUES

Musashi learned the kenjutsu Enmei-ryu that was created by his grandfather, Miyamoto Musashi no kami Yoshimoto. Musashi lived in the chaotic Warring States Period, a violent time during which only the strong survived, when warriors were at the pinnacle of society, and when Bushido and the common people's culture were born.

In his late years, Musashi changed the name of the ryuha from Enmei-ryu to Nito ichi-ryu, and two years before he passed away he changed the name of the ryuha again to Niten ichi-ryu. The niten (two skies), refers to the sun and the moon that revolve in the sky, based on the principle of yin and yang. In the right hand the long sword represents the sun, and the short sword held in the left hand represents the moon. The left and right are like the sun and the moon, and through the influence of this metaphor the name of the ryuha was chosen, lending it an astrological depth.

Musashi was a man of many skills. He tirelessly devoted himself to rigorous training in swordsmanship, but in addition to being a great swordsman he was also a strategist, and an artist who continually sought to create and develop new things. He was a truly gifted man. It is said that he was talented from birth, and that such a talented person like Musashi appears only once in every generation.

Nonetheless, in the case of kenjutsu and other crafts, the lineage is not limited only to family; students can inherit the tradition, refine it, and pass it on. The techniques, like D.N.A., continue until a new talent arrives and makes a contribution to improve them. Even in these days this theory is still relevant.

I began the study of Musashi's Niten ichi-ryu twenty years ago and continue to research its technique until this day. I have studied all the secret techniques of this ryuha directly from the ninth successor of Higohonden Yuhopo tenichi-ryu, Yonehara Kameo soke (Musashi was the first).

Nineteen years of age separate Yonehara Kameo soke and me, so when Yonehara started to guide me it felt like a father and son relationship. In the same way as Musashi's father passed the Enmei-ryu to his son, the Niten ichi-ryu techniques will be passed on, thanks to the kindness of Yonehara soke.

Historic Pictures

Portrait of Musashi, wearing a red vest. The interesting thing about this portrait is that although Musashi is standing in Gedan no kamae, his belt is too thin to hold two swords.

Authentic portrait of the literary and military arts genius, Miyamoto Musashi.

Master Santo Kiyotake, the 7th head master of Niten ichi-ryu.
This rare photograph from about 120 years ago is printed for the frst time in this book.

Master Aoki Kikuo, the 8th Soke.

Hidariwaki no kamae by Master Kameo Yonehara, the 9th Soke.

Jodan no kamae.

Starting from greeting and then Itto kenjutsu (one-sword techniques), receiving instruction of the mojiri gamae kenpo

1

2

3

4

5

6

7

8

9

First, before starting the practice of the innermost sword techniques, an outdoor greeting is performed.

In Niten ichi-ryu the basic Chudan no kamae is the Seigan no kamae, and according to the situation it is possible to change to two kinds of mojiri gamae. Within these kamae are the secret techniques.

In Seigan no kamae, the right leg steps forward and the sword is held straight. To change to mojiri gamae, step forward with the left leg and execute hanmi, holding the sword a little diagonally.

Picture 3: First step with the left leg.

Picture 4: The posture of mojiri gamae.

Picture 5: In order to be able to take control of the attacking enemy's sword the key is a subtle balance between the body and the sword.

Pictures 6-9: The secret of this kamae is the height of the point of the blade, and also receiving instructions on the movement of both hands. From this kamae you can conduct the secret technique of aisen uchidome; this technique will be shown later in this book.

Itto kenjutsu.
Receiving instructions for Seigan no kamae, Hasso no kamae, and Zanshin no kamae

1

2

3

4

5

6

Zanshin no kamae.

After an intense fight the body ceases to be in combat mode, but there is a chance that an enemy is still hiding. After confirming that there are no more potential enemies the mind goes back to its calm state, the dignified peaceful state of mind known as zanshin. This practice is performed commonly in demonstrations.
Picture 1: Listening to the explanation of this zanshin.
Pictures 2-3: Seigan no kamae.
Pictures 4-5: Hasso no kamae, following the teacher's instructions.

Itto kenjutsu. Aisen uchidome

1

2

3

4

5

6

7

Uchidachi (assailant) stands in Hasso no kamae, shitachi (counter-attacker) in mojiri gamae.
Uchidachi attacks straight form the top, shitachi lifts his kisaki (the point of the sword's blade) and grabs the partner's long sword, and while the sword comes down, pushes it to the left.
Then, when uchidachi tries to return to the original stance (hasso), shitachi attacks the face, ending the kata.

Itto kenjutsu. Technique that applies to chudan. The ukegaeshi no kata

1

2

3

4

5

6

7

8

Pictures 1-3: From aichudan, uchidachi changes to Hasso no kamae. The change is executed swiftly without giving even a split-second opening.
Pictures 4-8: Shitachi steps back one step and changes to gedan without kamae. Uchidachi attacks straight from Hasso no kamae. Shitachi blocks the attack and lets it slide, and then attacks the face.

Itto kenjutsu. Sassen no kata

1

4

2

5

3

6

Pictures 1-3: Both parties start in aiseigan and take one step back. Uchidachi changes to hasso, shitachi changes to koshi gamae. Then, when uchidachi attacks from the front, shitachi takes one step forward with his right leg and stabs uchidachi in the neck or the side. If stabbing with the movement of the arm, the sufficient result may not be achieved, therefore it is better to first stretch the arm and then with a step forward stab the partner. In Pictures 4-6 the technique was tried against a full armored warrior who is holding a spear. In that case, after the opponent drops the spear, stab the side of the neck.

Itto kenjutsu. Toraburi no kata

1

2

3

4

5

6

7

8

Picture 1: Being taught the Toraburi no kamae.
Pictures 2-4: Uchidachi stands in Hasso no kamae, shitachi starts in Torafuri no kamae. Uchidachi attacks the front, shitachi, while taking a right step forward, cuts uchidachi's neck.
Pictures 6-8: Against an armored warrior holding a spear.
First, shitachi stands in Toraburi no kamae. When uchidachi attacks with the spear, shitachi uses the blade to divert the spear and then cuts the neck.

Itto kenjutsu. Haritsuke no kata

1

2

3

4

5

6

To deflect a sword striking at high speed is difficult, but not impossible, so shitachi should use his left hand and hold the back of his sword. When shitachi starts to block uchidachi's sword in jodan, he sticks both of the swords together, then drops the swords to the left side. When uchidachi pulls back to jodan in order to strike again, shitachi enters with both hands on the sword. End of kata.

This was one of the techniques that Musashi refined. It is a very difficult technique, and requires a very high level of skill to perform.

Kodachi (short sword). Seigan no kata

1

2

3

4

5

6

Shitachi starts from gedan, and with the right hand lifts the sword as if trying to stab the eyes of uchidachi with the tip of the sword. Uchidachi strikes in order to try to cut the hand, shitachi drops his right hand and while removing uchidahi's sword steps forward with the right leg, and cuts uchidachi's wrist. Shitachi takes another step forward with the left leg and holds uchidachi's arm, with todome no kata (a fatal blow.) End of technique.

Kodachi. Sassen no kata

1

2

3

This kata is the same as the sasen with one long sword. While uchidachi strikes, shitachi takes one step to the side with the right leg, and stabs the neck.

Kodachi. Ukenagashi no kata

1

2

3

4

5

6

7

8

This kata has the same points as the ukenagashi with the long sword. Shitachi fends off the attack of uchidachi and slices the side of the neck. With the left hand shitachi grabs the hilt of uchidachi's sword thus preventing him from using his sword freely, and stabs. End of kata.

Receiving instructions of Nito Seiho (two swords kenjutsu), Gedan no kamae

1

2

3

4

5

6

7

Picture 1: Yonehara soke demonstrating Gedan no kamae.
Pictures 2-4: Receiving detailed instructions about the stretch of the arm or the angle of the wrist when standing in Gedan.
Picture 5: While doing Gedan no kamae the swords should be pointing out but not without an opening.
Picture 6: Gedan no kamae.

Trying in two forms to put to real practice the Ryusui technique

The first version of Ryusui—Ogi no tachi

1

2

3

4

5

6

The Ogi no tachi technique is a sword technique that has been refined to a very high level. Shitachi (holding two swords) stands in Gedan no kamae, uchidachi stands in hasso and strikes. Shitachi uses the left hand holding the kodachi to block uchidachi's sword by touching it from the outer side, sliding it to the inner part, and then pushing it down. At the same time with the right hand lifting the sword and striking to the center.

The second version of Ryusui, "Aikuchi shikata no koto"

1

2

3

This technique is referred to by the same name, and this is also a very advanced technique. Yonehara soke passes this technique only at shihan level. Shitachi (holding two swords) stands in Gedan no kamae, and uchidachi stabs with one hand. Shitachi, with the left hand holding the kodachi, blocks the strike from the inner side pushing to the outer side, at the same time lifting the long sword to jodan and striking the center.

Receiving instructions about Migiwaki no kata

1

2

3

4

5

Pictures 1, 2: Yonehara soke demonstrates Migiwaki no kamae.
Pictures 3, 4: Receiving instructions about the best angle to hold the kodachi so that the enemy cannot attack.
Picture 5: The author stands in Migiwaki no kamae.

Techniques from Gedan (mugamae)

1

2

3

4

5

This Gedan is not a kamae; this stance is called Mugamae (non-kamae), but frankly this is a high-level stance; its purpose is to draw the opponent's attack. When shitachi stands in Gedan, all the upper part of the body is open so it is certain that uchidachi will always attack from above. Shitachi takes one step back and removes the attack, and then he lifts both of the swords to jo-dan and immediately blocks again, pushing uchidachi's sword with the kodachi, and with the long sword he strikes the center.

Combining two techniques together, a practice for actual fights

1

2

3

4

5

6

7

8

In Niten ichi-ryu, when progressing in practice, in order to improve one's skills, practices in which two techniques are combined also take place.
Pictures 1-5: Uchidachi stabs with one hand, then shitachi uses Igeta kenpo to block and immediately uses the Koyo technique to drop uchidachi's sword.
Pictures 6-8: Uchidachi tightens the hold of his sword and stands in Hasso no kamae. Shitachi changes to Migiwaki no kamae.
From here uchidachi attacks the right hand so shitachi cuts the torso and then strikes the center. End of technique. This technique combines the migiwaki technique and the koyo technique together.

Koyo no kata

1

Shitachi (holding two swords) stands in Hidariwaki no kamae. Uchidachi stabs, and shitachi, using the kodachi, blocks the strike with an up-down movement, and then pushes the sword outside. With the right hand holding the long sword he knocks uchidachi's sword down. This is a very powerful technique.

2

3

4

5

6

7

In Musashi's later years it was the end of the war period, times of peace prevailed, and many warriors started working as administrative officials for the government. Musashi, combining the tastes of royalty and warriors, created this ryuha from the powerful kenjutsu techniques and refined aspects of traditional Noh theater, and, eliminating any wasteful parts during the refining process, passed it on as an art. Nevertheless, the original koyo technique is a very fierce one, and the powerful side of this ryuha is clearly visible.

CHAPTER 2

Rivals of Musashi

SHINKAGE-RYU KENJUTSU

The government in the Muromachi Period (around 1500) was known for its political incapability. During these times the values of society had started to change, largely from the influence of the internal wars that were spreading. Times came in which warriors started looking for techniques that would raise their status, combining fighting with the search for superior knowledge, instead of pure techniques that considered nothing but the actual fight itself.

In those times, Matsumoto Bizen no kami Ki no Masamoto, a Shinto priest of the Kashima Shrine and a military general, had been studying the Katori shinto-ryu and the Kashima sword techniques; from these techniques he developed the Kashima shin-ryu. Many great warriors studied under the instruction of Matsumoto Bizen no kami, warriors like Tsuhara Bokuden. One such student was a young general named Kamiizumi Hidetsuna (Nobutsuna). Kamiizumi had studied under Bizen no kami, and had been taught all the inner secrets of his sword techniques. After finishing his studies under Matsumoto Bizen no kami, he studied the Kage-ryu, and during these studies he had a revelation. He decided to merge his experiences of the battlefield with his studies of the Kami shin-ryu and Kage-ryu, and developed a new ryuha, the Shinkage-ryu.

Kamiizumi Nobutsuna held the high rank "Iseno kami," and he felt very blessed to be such a highly ranked warrior. Only those who were very intelligent, good looking, well mannered, and with excellently conditioned bodies came to study in his school, and for this reason the Shinkage-ryu gained great reputation as a style and had a very big influence on the Japanese Kenpo world.

Evidence of its great influence is the enormous amount of other ryuha that developed from the Shinkage-ryu, including the Taisha-ryu, Jiki shinkage-ryu, Oishi Shinkage-ryu, Muraku-ryu, Muso-ryu, and many more. Many of history's great warriors studied this ryuha, and it had a great influence on Bushido and

Musashi visits Hyogonosuke. First of all they exchange greetings.

This picture shows Musashi visiting his friend Yagyu Hyogonosuke. They exchange greetings and then exchange techniques between the Shinkage-ryu and Niten ichi-ryu.

The Shinkage-ryu bow etiquette. In a match or a demonstration, the warrior conducts a bow called soko.
This is the first time that the Shinkage-ryu's fully armed sword techniques have been published. This is in order to show evidence that these techniques were useful also in the battlefield.

became a main school in the kenjutsu world. One of the legitimate successors of the Shinkage-ryu was Yagiyu Muneyoshi (Sekishusai). The grandson of Yagiyu Muneyoshi, Yagyu Hyogonosuke, followed in his grandfather's footsteps as the head of the Yagyu family and succeeded the ryuha. He became the kejutsu teacher of the Tokugawa family that was located in the Owari area; they were from the same family as the shogun, and this part of the Yagyu family became the Owari Yagyu.

Furthermore, Yagyu Muneyoshi's fifth son, Yagyu Munenori, was recommended as a kenjutsu teacher to the first shogun Iyeasu Tokugawa. He was also the teacher of the second shogun Hidetada, and the third Iemitsu. Not only in kenjutsu did Munenori have many achievements; he achieved much on the political stage as well. He became very famous and the Shinkage-ryu became Japan's preeminent ryuha.

This family was called the Edo Yagyu. Although this style is often called Yagyu shinkage-ryu, its original name is simply Shinkage-ryu. The Yagyu family became very powerful, and as Munenori was the kenjutsu teacher of the Tokugawa shogunate and their relatives in Owari, the Shinkage-ryu became very famous for its kenjutsu and the strategy methods, as did the Yagyu family, who in order to maintain this status had to foster considerable mental power.

On a side note, the Yagyu-ryu body and mind secret techniques, which were written by Yagyu Munenori of the Edo Yagyu family, called *The Life-giving Sword* has been printed by Kodansha International in 2003 and in order to understand this history better, it is recommended the reader refer to this book.

Unfortunately, these days the Edo shinkage-ryu has disappeared, but the legitimate Owari shikage-ryu has been passed on to a group called Marobashikai, which is still active today. The president of the Marobashikai,Tadashige Watanabe, and I have been good friends for many years, therefore while receiving instruction about the secret techniques of Shinkage-ryu, the research is continuing. In this ryuha, the main object of the techniques, the killing, is carefully hidden; it is passed on today as a kenjutsu strategy that can take place in a peaceful society as a means to educate people.

Itto ryodan

A picture from a makimono of the Edo period.

Itto Ryodan no kata, performed by armored soldiers.

1

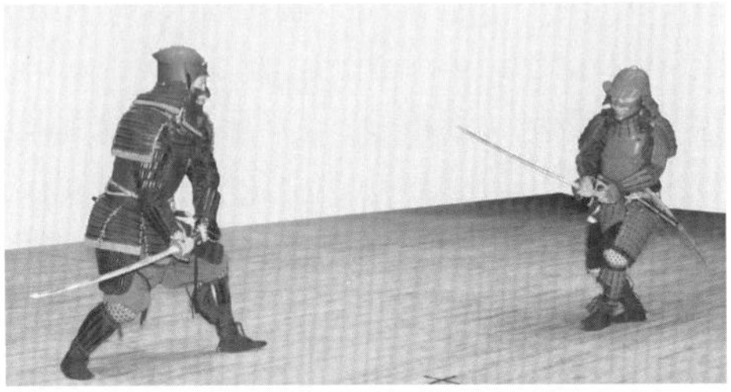

2

3

4

An armored style from the front.

5

6

An armored style from the side.

Itto Ryodan no kata, performed in kimono.

1

2

3

4

5

6

7

8

9

The meaning of the name of this technique is to cut the opponent in two. The party on the left holding the sword stands in Kuruma no kamae, and by doing this he shows the opponent his left shoulder. The right party, aiming towards this shoulder or the arm, attacks from above. Then, the left party strikes the opponent's wrist so the left shoulder will be safe. Once seeing his attack has failed the right party changes the stance to jodan to strike again, and without separating the sword the left party strikes the left wrist again. End of technique.

Zantei Saitetsu

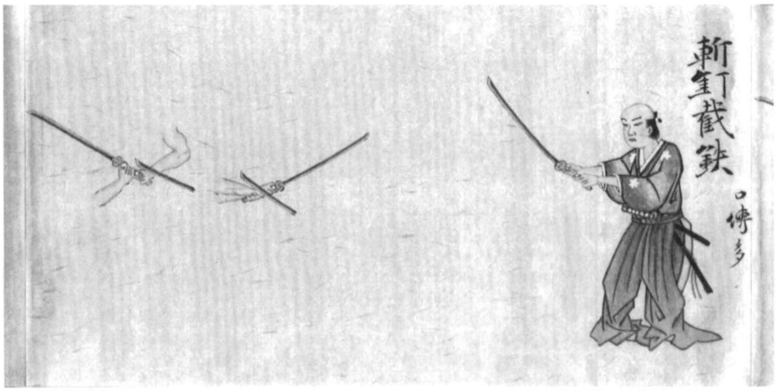

A picture from a makimono.

Zantei Saitetsu no kata in armor.

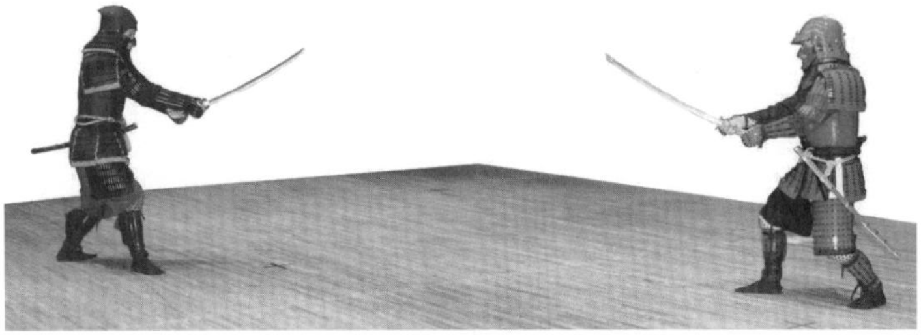
1

2

3

4

5

6

7

Zantei Saitetsu no kata in kimono.

1

2

3

4

5

6

7

The meaning of the name of this technique is to cut a spike or an iron stick. The left partner stands in Segan no kamae, this is like a spike or an iron stick being used as a shield and hiding one's body behind it. If there is even a small opening then the right partner will attack, then hit the partner's sword close to its edge (9 cm) and then strike his right wrist. While the partner backs to Jodan no kamae, without separating the sword strike his left wrist. End of technique.

Hankai hanko

An illustration in a makimono.

Hankai hanko no kata in armor.

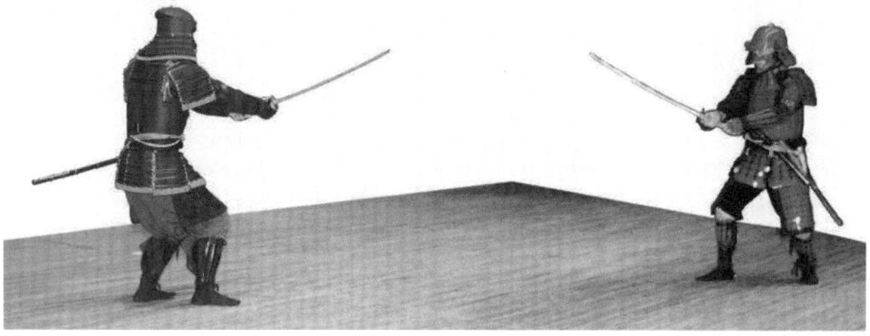

1

2

3

4

5

6

7

Hankai hanko no kata in kimono.

1

2

3

4

5

6

7

In this technique, when the partner strikes, move the left leg under the partner's right hand and open the body half way. Looking carefully at the partner's right grip, hit the center of his hilt. While the partner backs to Jodan no kamae, without separating strike his left wrist. End of technique.

Usen saten

The illustrations of Saten usen (left) and Usen saten.

Usen saten no kata in armor.

1

2

3

4

5

6

7

Usen saten no kata in kimono.

1

2

3

4

5

Chotan ichimi

In this technique, when the partner strikes move to the left and strike his right wrist, then again toward the partner's strike move to the right side and strike the center of his hilt. End of technique.

1

2

3

4

5

In this technique the sword is stretched like a long spear. The inner secret of this technique is that even if one doesn't stretch the sword it is possible to win. When the duel comes to a point when both sides can't move, as shown in Picture 1, lower the sword, and change to Gedan no kamae. doing that gives an opening of the right shoulder, the partner will attack aiming to that shoulder, then, as shown in Pictures 3 and 4, stretch the arm and hit in the partner's hilt. End of technique.

Kaboku no kata, drawn from kuka no tachi (the nine sword techniques)

1

2

3

4

5

6

The meaning of kaboku is to employ a soft way in order to win over the opponent. When the partner doesn't attack, this side starts the technique in order to make him attack. (The inner secret is that because the opponent's hand becomes stiff he doesn't attack, then with a soft move this side makes him attack.) Next, strike the left wrist, from that pose pull the partner closer. End of technique.

Receiving instructions on the inner secrets of the way of striking

1

2

3

4

5

This technique is the basic strike of Shinkage-ryu, but despite this it is also a closely guarded secret.
Both sides stand in jodan and strike so the swords will meet; the stronger side with the power of the strike pushes aside the partner's sword and hits the wrist. End of technique.

Shinkage-ryu's ryoto (two swords) no kamae

1

2

3

These two-sword techniques are based on Musashi's Enmei-ryu Nito ken.

Receiving instructions on the ryoto techniques

1

2

3

4

5

6

7

8

9

Ukyo Tanaka is being instructed by Watanabe Shoshu. From Gedan enkyoku no kamae, lifting both of the swords, then changing the stance to Chudan enkyo no kamae.

Shinkage-ryu's ryoto (Shishi no horairi)

1

2

3

4

5

6

7

8

Shitachi stands in Chudan enkyoku no kamae, uchidachi starts from Segan no kamae and changes to Jodan no kamae and strikes. Shitachi uses the two swords to press down from the upper side, and then stabs the throat. End of technique.

Niten ichi-ryu's double arm cutting from chudan

1

2

Using the Niten ichi-ryu double arm cutting chudan sword technique against the Shinkage-ryu's strike.

Niten ichi-ryu's toraburi to attack two swords

1

2

Using the Niten ichi-ryu's toraburi sword technique to strike down the Shinkage-ryu's Chudan enkyoku no kamae.

SHINAKAGE-RYU'S NITO YABURI

Miyamoto Musashi and Hyogonosuke from Owari Yagyu were good friends, and they set themselves the goals of seeking the secrets of kenjutsu, and exchanging knowledge. One day, when Musashi was walking in the streets of Nagoya, he met Hyogonosuke by chance. Hyogonosuke invited Musashi to stay in the Yagyu residence and teach the two-sword techniques of Enmei-ryu. During this time Musashi also studied the Shinkage-ryu techniques. After Musashi left, Hyogonosuke developed techniques to defeat the nito kenpo; these techniques are known as the nito yaburi. They have been passed on as secret techniques for 400 years until today. Here I can introduce some katas with the help of SoshuWatanabe.

Nito yaburi no.1

1

2

3

4

5

6

7

8

The two-sword party stands in Chudan no kamae, the right starts from Seigan and moves to Gedan, and lifts the opponent's daito, and immediately steps with the left leg forward and strikes the right wrist. End of technique.

Nito yaburi no.2

1

2

3

4

5

6

7

8

9

The two-sword party stands in Migi jodan no kamae, the right party stands in hasso and approaches. Swiftly he strikes the opponent's left wrist. The two-sword party strikes with the long sword, then the right party takes one step to the right and strikes the sword from the left and again strikes the left wrist. End of technique.

Nito yaburi no.3

1

2

3

4

5

The two-sword party stands in Migi jodan no kamae, the right party stands in hasso and approaches. Swiftly he strikes the opponent's left wrist. The two-sword party strikes with the long sword, then the right party takes one step to the right and strikes the sword from the left and again strikes the left wrist. End of technique.

TODA-RYU'S SHORT SWORD

The Toda-ryu was founded in the 16th century during the Warring States Period and became famous for its short sword techniques that are efficient in real battle. The Toda-ryu got its name from the warrior Toda Seigen. It is said that Miyamoto Musashi's defeated rival, Sasaki Kojiro, was the disciple of Toda Seigen. While Toda Seigen was researching techniques with the short sword (kodachi), Sasaki Kojiro served as his partner using a special sword. It is not known exactly when, but at some point Kojiro became skilled with the long sword (odachi) and started his own ryuha; the Iwao-ryu. This story has many contradictions, however, so I have attempted to verify its authenticity. Today, in the Tsugaru region in Aomori prefecture in northern Japan, there is a person who carries the name of Toda-ryu. I made several attempts to contact him in order to gather material, but did not receive a reply. I heard about a large Budo gathering in the area so I attended, hoping to collect some material, but we had only a brief greeting before he fled away. Incidentally, the name of their ryuha is Touda-ryu and not Toda-ryu, as is traditionally pronounced. The group in northern Japan says that they got the pictorial scroll of the Toda-ryu from the descendant of the Asari family in Yokohama, but I hold the copy of the scroll and I have been researching the technique. What follows is a demonstration of the techniques with my students.

A portrait of Toda Seigen, from the Edo period.

Techniques

Tobi chigai

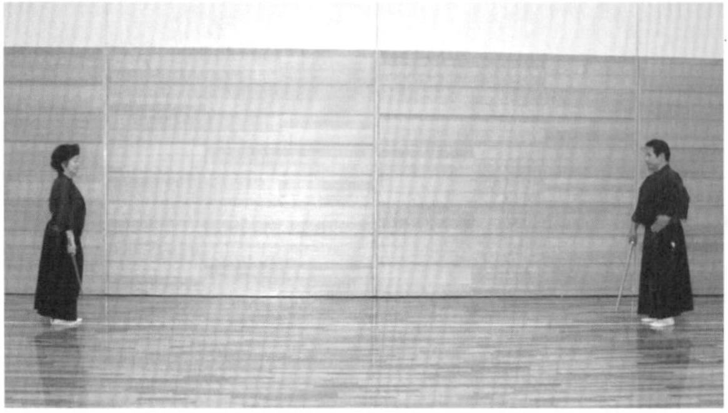
1

2

3

4

5

6

Uchidachi holds a long sword; shitachi holds a short sword. Uchidachi stands in jodan Hasso no kamae, shitachi stands in Fudo no kamae. Both parties run to each other, uchidachi attacks straight to the face, so shitachi, while turning his body left, lifts the hand holding the sword above the head, tilts the uchidachi's sword to the side, and then cuts him diagonally. End of technique. Both parties hold the sword in one hand in Gedan, and without doing kamae they assume zanshin.

Tsubazuri (ryote gaeshi)

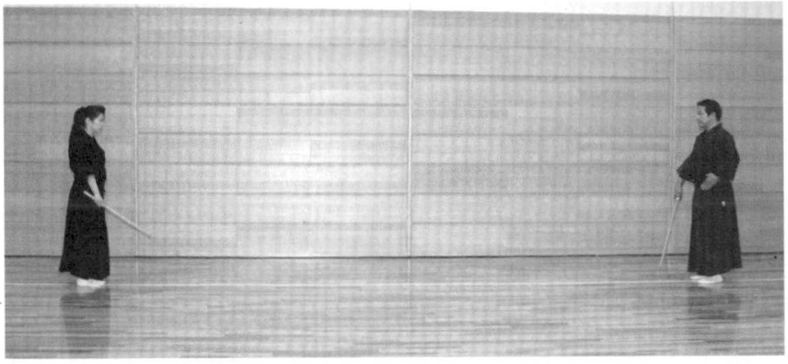
1

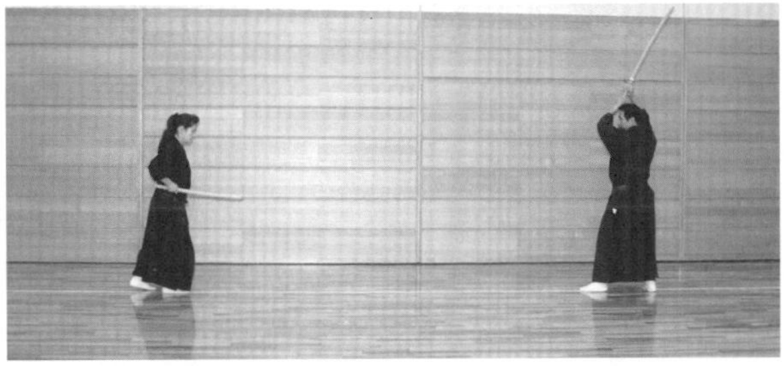
2

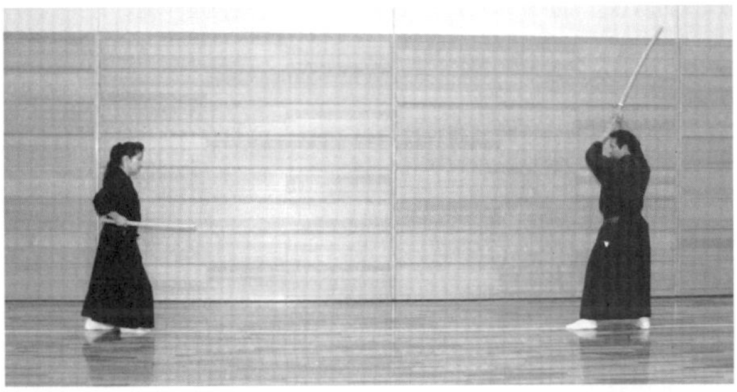
3

4

5

6

7

Uchidachi stands in Hasso no kamae. Shitachi holds the sword in one hand and stands in Gedan mugamae (no kamae). While Uchidachi keeps the Hasso no kamae and faces shitachi, shitachi places his short sword in the right side of his waist and changes to tsuki no kame. Both sides step towards each other. Uchidachi attacks straight and shitachi holds with both hands the short sword and directs uchidachi to the side. Then she takes a big step with the right foot and cuts the right side of the neck. End of technique. Both parties hold their swords in one hand, stand in mugamae, and assume zanshin.

Issoku fukyo

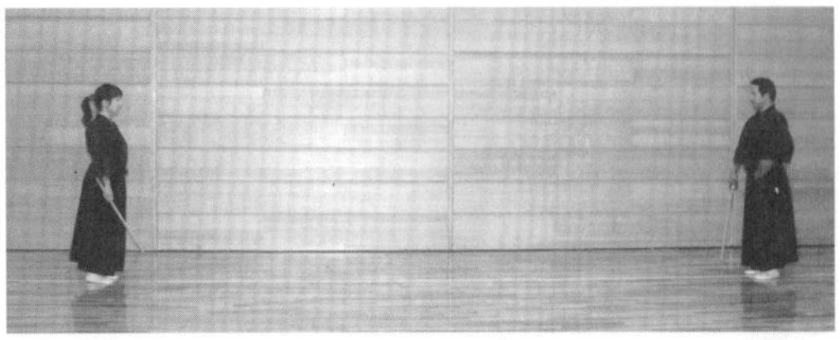
1

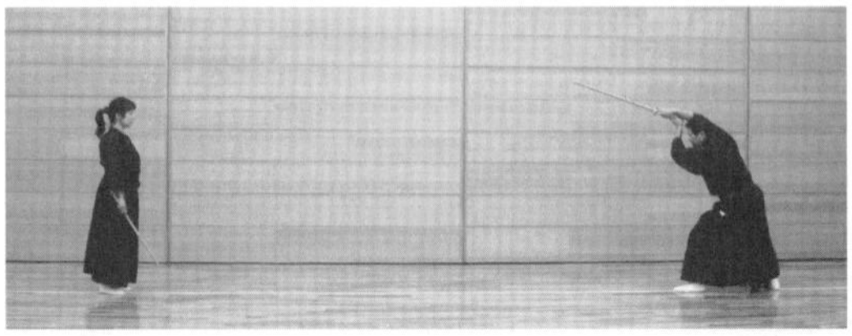
2

3

4

5

6

7

8

9

Uchidachi stands in Kasumi no kamae, shitachi holds the sword in one hand and stands without kamae. Both parties walk towards each other. Uchidachi keeps his Kasumi no kamae, shitachi holds the sword with both hands and stands in Seigan no kamae. Both lift their swords a little so shitachi assumes the posture of jodan seigan, and gets closer to uchidachi. Suddenly, uchidachi changes his stance to jodan and attacks from above. Shitachi stabs with the short sword and catches the shinugi (the side of the blade) of uchidachi's sword with the short sword pushing the sword to the left, then steps forward with the right leg and pushes the sword further left. Shitachi, using the reaction of uchidachi, cuts the partner's neck from left to right. End of technique. Both parties hold their swords with one hand and assume zanshin.

IWAO-RYU (GANRYU)

Iwao-ryu is a ryuha that was founded by Sasaki Kojiro in the 16th century, who fought with Miyamoto Musashi on Funashima (Ganryu Island).

Sasaki Kojiro died in that duel, but the style that he taught, Iwao-ryu, was passed on secretly in Satsuma (today Kagoshima prefecture) and Higo (today Kumamoto prefecture). Particularly in Higo, the fighting and mental techniques were passed on until the end of the Meiji Era (around 1912).

In Kumamoto prefecture, after 300 years had passed the successors of Miyamoto Musashi and Sasaki Kojiro had reached an historical understanding and made good relationships between the ryuhas. This meant that the 7th soke of Miyamoto Musashi's Niten ichi-ryu, Santo Kiyotake, started to learn the secret techniques from the successors of the Iwao-ryu in the middle of the Meiji Era (1868-1912), and after him his successor, the 8th soke of Niten ichi-ryu, Aoki Tesshin.

This is evidence of how the two ryuhas have fostered good relations. I heard this story from Yonehara Kameo Shihan, the 9th soke of Sekiguchi-ryu iaijutsu and Niten ichi-ryu (also, Santo and Aoki soke were in charge on both of the ryuhas).

Around 1950, the successors of Iwao-ryu and Yonehara Kameo Shihan both lived in Kumamoto city in the Hakusan area, therefore exchange of information became frequent, as they shared with each other various scrolls and books. Also, Yonehara Shihan had a chance to see a boken (wooden sword) that was slightly different from the standard sword used in bujutsu (martial arts). This boken looked the same as the sword of the esoteric Buddhist god Fudomyo'o and is called ganryubo.

An acquaintance of mine, Mr. Kimura, had heard of the existence of this boken and made a special entreatment to the successors of Iwao-ryu to make a copy of it. I contacted Mr. Kimura and was able to buy one of the only few remaining ganryubo. The boken is portrayed in the pictures on page 91.

In 2008 I went to Kumamoto, and in Kumamoto Castle, re-enacted the Iwao-ryu techniques under the guidance of Yonehara Shihan. (See illustrations on page 92.)

The character of Sasaki Kojiro is shrouded in a lot of mystery; for example where he was born. Many inaccuracies also surround him; for example the fact that the name of the ryuha he founded is today called Ganryu, but its real name is Iwao-ryu. Moreover, it is said that he was a student of Toda Seigen of the Toda-ryu, but if this is true, it means that when he fought with Musashi he would have been over seventy years old; obviously not an age for duelling. Also, in the novel

Musashi and in various movies the character of Sasaki is described as a handsome young man; there isn't any clear proof of this fact either.

When the author saw this boken it suggested to him that Sasaki Kojiro wasn't at all like the person who is described in the popular novel. Sasaki Kojiro was deeply involved in an esoteric Buddhist group, and because he held a leader stance in this group he was called the ganryubo (the ganryu preist), or Sasaki Ganryu.

There are old writings that say that the duel between Miyamoto Musashi and Sasaki Kojiro took place on Funashima (Ganryu Island) on 13th April, 1612. There was an agreement that it would be a one-on-one duel without the presence of any students. Despite this, it is said that one of Musashi's students secretly came and hid out of sight. Musashi won the duel, but Kojiro didn't die instantly, so Musashi's student dealt the finishing blow. Even if this outcome wasn't according to Musashi's wish, he had broken the agreement, and after the duel Kojiro's students wanted to kill Musashi. He fled to Nagato (today Yamaguchi prefecture), and lived under the protection of an influential man.

Furthermore, it is said that Kojiro was very good in the kenjutsu technique tsubame gaeshi, but this technique existed in other kenjutsu techniques in Japan before the Iwao-ryu was founded. Also, today, ryuha like Tenshin Shodenka Torishinto-ryu and Kukamin shin-ryu, as well as other styles, are teaching this technique. It is not clear if it is a technique that was created by Sasaki Kojiro. The people who hold the Iwao-ryu's scrolls, books, and ganryubo (the boken) have moved from Kumamoto City and have disappeared without a trace. But from what I hear, research on this matter is still in progress.

The wooden sword of Iwao-ryu is called Ganryubo.

1

2

3

4

5

6

7

The ganryubo is the same shape as the sword of the esoteric Buddhist god Fudomyo'o.
The author stands in kamae (posture) with the ganryubo.
The re-enactment of the tsubame gaeshi technique under the guidance of eighty-seven-year-old soke Yanehara Kameo, who learned it from Santo Kiyotake and Aoki Tesshin.
First, the author lies on the ground on his right side. The instant he grabs the sword hilt, he quickly draws the sword to his right, and immediately jumps to his right and vertically cuts the enemy. The author is sixty-six years old, so obviously it was problematic to execute the technique quickly.

SHINTO MUSO-RYU

This style was developed by Muso Gonnosuke. He studied the Kashima shinto-ryu and Katori Shinto-ryu and reached in his studies the inner secrets of the ryuha. When he embarked on his Musha Shugyo (a pilgrimage in order to study), he fought Miyamoto Musashi with a roku saku (1.8m) bujutsu and lost. After this incident, he became Musashi's student.

Some time later Gonnosuke retreated to a shrine in the depths of the mountains and prayed to the gods. In order to develop new techniques he followed a very strict training. One day he received the advice of a god: the sword is used in order to kill, but the stick is not so deadly. He quickly had an idea for a new weapon—a 4 shaku 2 sun 1 bu (128cm)-long stick known as the jo.

After that he duelled again with Musashi and it is said that with his new technique he won the duel. Gonnosuke was instructed by Musashi to create a new, splendid ryuha, so he took the secret techniques of Shindo-ryu, and he received godly guidance in a dream (in Japanese *muso*) and was able to complete the jo technique, so he named his ryuha Shinto Muso-ryu.

Following this incident he became a vassal of a daimyo called Kuroda clan, and many warriors were able to study this ryuha. These days it is practiced by aikido and kendo practitioners, and also by the police.

The material gathered for these ryuha was possible thanks to the kindness of Matsuda Shigeharu Shihan (Shinto Muso-ryu 8th dan hanshi). Matsuda Shihan and I have also studied together the Kuki shin-ryu Bujutsu techniques, and he has become a sworn brother to me.

A portrait of Muso Gonnosuke, drawn in the Edo period.

Techniques

(All the techniques presented in this book are advanced-level techniques)

Aun

1

2

3

4

5

6

7

8

9

10

11

12

Picture 1: The sword party stands in Seigan no kamae, the jo party in Tsune no kamae.
Pictures 2-7: The sword party moves to hasso and strikes, the jo party moves to hiki-otoshi no kame and blocks the sword. He immediately pulls down the jo, and then using a technique called honde uchi he knocks away the sword to the right.
Pictures 9-12: The jo party lifts the jo above the head and strikes with the suigetsu strike.
Picture 13: Assume zanshin.

Suigetsu —the kata which defeated Miyamoto Musashi

The movements of the Nito (two swords) party.

1

2

3

4

5

6

7

8

Pictures 1-3: Changing from Gedan no kamae to Migi jodan no kamae.
Picture 5: Blocking the jo hitting down by crossing two swords.
Pictures 6-7: Suppressing the jo hitting up by decussating two swords.

Kime no kata

1

2

3

4

5

6

7

8

At the end of the technique the kime no kata is used. The enduring techniques of the Shinto-ryu that the founder Muso Gonosuke practiced are studied, and the teachings of the gods that he received in his dreams have become the influence of the techniques ending with striking to the right side and then stabbing with a suigetsu. It is also said that it is possibly this technique that knocked down Musashi's swords.

Suigetsu no kata

The two-sword movement (Miyamoto Musashi)

1

2

3

4

5

6

7

8

9

10

11

Picture 1: Standing in Gedan no kamae.
Picture 3: Changing to Migi jodan no kamae.

Picture 6: Crossing the swords and blocking the jo.
Pictures 8-11: The two swords are pushing the jo.

The jo against sword kata

12

13

14

15

16

17

18

19

20

21

22

This is the technique which beat Musashi's two-swords kenpo.
The person on the right represents Muso Gonnosuke, on the left is Miyamoto Musashi.
Picture 1: Gonnosuke stands in Tsune no kamae, Musashi stands in Gedan no mukamae.
Pictures 2-5: Musashi points out the kodachi and then crosses both of the swords and stands in Chudan no kamae. Gonnosuke watches carefully.
Pictures 6-8: Musashi approaches while standing in Chudan no kamae, so Gonnosuke knocks down the crossed swords from above.
Pictures 8-15: Musashi opens both his swords to the right and left, dodges the jo's strike, and pushes the jo down with both swords.
Pictures 16-21: Gonnosuke, who's being pushed by Musashi's swords, puts his jo in a vertical position and avoids the pushing of the swords. He falls to the ground and immediately strikes the center. Musashi crosses his swords again in a jujidome and blocks the strike. Again, Gonnosuke puts his jo in a vertical position and pushes the swords up, then with hidari no kobushi (left hand fist) hits Musashi's solar plexus, touches the ground with one knee, and strikes again to the solar plexus. End of technique.

MUSASHI'S TWO-SWORD TECHNIQUES AGAINST A SPEAR

If Musashi were to fight against a spear, the author believes that using two swords is the best strategy, so based on the research of ryuha that are related to Musashi, such as the Niten ichi-ryu, Shinkage-ryu, Shingyoto-ryu, and the Yagyu-ryu, the author tried to re-enact techniques of two swords against a spear.

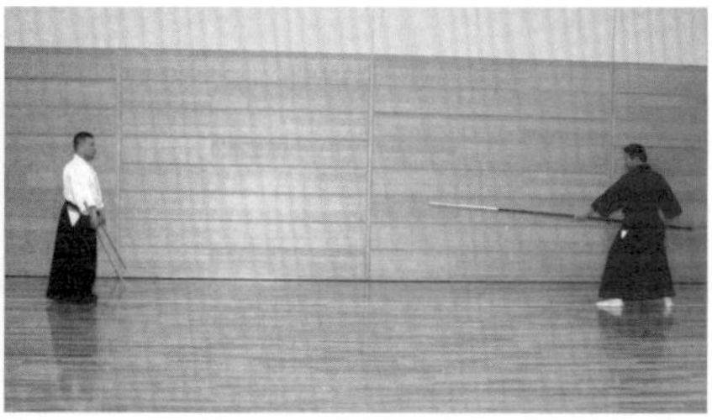
1

2

3

4

5

6

7

8

9

Techniques
The party holding the two swords starts in Gedan, then he pulls his hands to the sides and opens the center. The party with the spear, from Chudan no kamae, tries to stab. The two-swords party crosses the swords and blocks and pushes the spear. The spear party lifts the spear up so that he pushes the swords. In order to attack the face, the two-swords party brings the swords down. The two-swords party crosses his swords in jodan and blocks the attack, then he knocks the spear down to the left, and while keeping the spear down slices to the neck. End of technique.

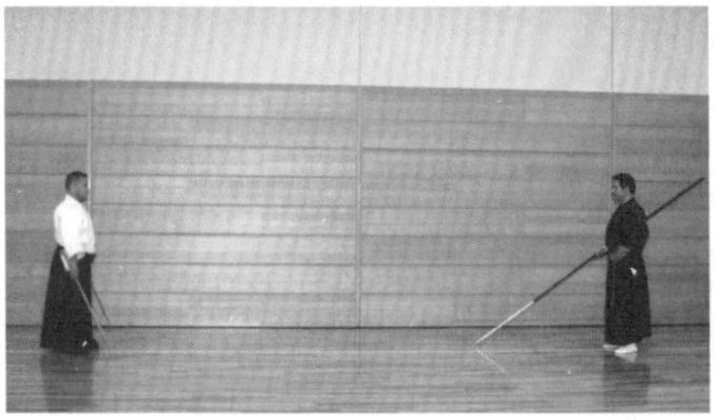

1

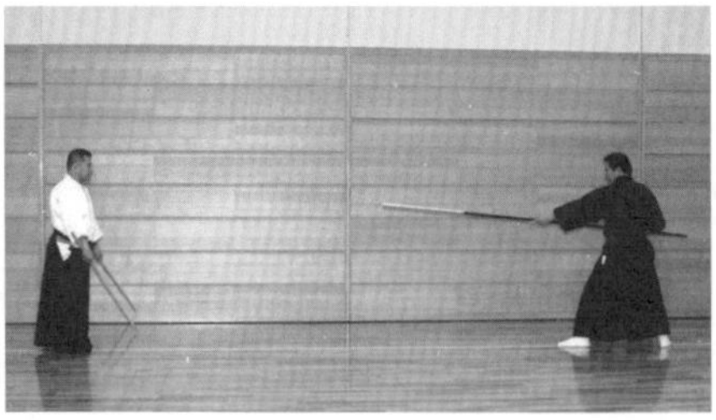

2

3

4

5

6

7

8

9

10

The two-swords party stands in Gedan and changes to migi jodan. While changing the stance the party holding the spear doesn't miss an opening and from a chudan attacks the face. The two-swords party blocks the spear with the kodachi in the left hand and immediately blocks the second strike with the daito. The party with the spear uses the force of the block to attack again with the blade-less side of the spear, and again the two-swords party blocks with the kodachi. The spear party switches the direction of the spear so the blade is once again in front, and attacks from above. The two-swords party blocks with the daito and slices the neck with the kodachi. End of technique.

HOZOIN-RYU TAKATA-HA SOJUTSU

The founder of this style was a Buddhist priest named Hozoin In'ei. He lived during the times of the internal wars of Japan and was profoundly affected by them—the temples in Nara were often attacked by robbers and mobs. While the warriors were occupied in going to battle, temples that were national treasures were set on fire, and a great deal of damage was inflicted in those days.

Putting aside their intentions of going to war or fighting for self-gain, the priests learned about martial arts and formed a troop of soldier-priests in order to protect the supporters and followers of the temple. Hozoin In'ei was the disciple of the Kamiizumi Ise no kami Nobutsuna, the founder of Shinkage-ryu kenjutsu, who travelled around Japan and taught this ryuha.

Kamiizumi Ise no kami Nobutsuna was a part of the Ohko clan that was located in Joshu (today Gunma prefecture). In those times during war the spear was considered to be a first-class weapon, and Kamiizumi Ise no kami was well known for his use of the spear. Not only that, he was also very knowledgeable of sword techniques against the spear. It is said that he had no rival in the use of the spear.

Hozoin In'ei became a student of Kamiizumi Ise no kami Nobutsuna, and he was influenced deeply by the guiding curriculum of the new-era Shinkage-ryu kenjutsu techniques. It is believed that besides the kenjutsu techniques he studied the actual battle spear techniques that Nobutsuna was retaining.

Around 1500, Daizendayu Moritada came to Hozoin In'ei temple to study the arts of the spear, and after hard practice they managed to develop techniques for a new weapon, the jumonji yari, and after developing a proper teaching system, the Hozoin-ryu was born.

Thanks to In'ei's fine character and the efforts of his students, the Hozoin-ryu became very famous. One day Miyamoto Musashi came to challenge this school as a part of his quest for glory, but on that day In'ei was out for errands, so one of his disciples fought Musashi and lost to him.

Concerning the result of that incident, novelists and common people made all kinds of violent stories, for example: that the priests couldn't handle the disgrace of losing and attacked Musashi by surprise, or that in the end In'ei had the duel with Musashi. Maybe within all these stories there might be some strands of truth.

Nevertheless, Buddhism is against killing and violence; the base of Buddhism is harmony. The Buddhist way of life is that priests must set an example to warriors and common people for a calm, reasonable way of life and good manners. In duels, even if a fierce duel employing high-level secret techniques is held, nobody's life is in danger—there isn't any use of real swords. The purpose of the duel and matches of this ryuha were different.

In addition, looking at Musashi's literary and military arts, it is possible to see that he wasn't a violent man who enjoyed killing. In'ei and the rest of his priest disciples used duels and matches as ways to progress in the techniques of the spear; there wasn't any room for hatred or grudge in the training. In'ei wouldn't duel even a first-class warrior, so it is natural that a nameless ronin like Musashi wouldn't have made a fit partner for In'ei and his students in training.

This ryuha, with its glorious long history, was distinct from the other ryuhas. The students of this ryuha were top-class warriors, but unfortunately, after the samurai period, in the modern age it came to be absorbed into competitive kendo and modern naginata; the classic techniques of this ryuha have vanished.

The people who held dear this ryuha memorized it by looking at the few techniques that were left, practicing them diligently to recreate the ryuha. These days, Kagita Chubei, who was a member of the Nara municipality and the Japanese parliament, is the 20th soke and is training new shihans to preserve and pass on this ryuha. This ryuha is a great example of preserving Japanese culture out of respect for its history and ancestors.

In this style, when practicing the techniques, a part of the blade called the hosako, which is positioned straight, and another hosako, which is horizontal, combine to make a "ju" sign, and have been used for many different kinds of practice. This spear is called kamayari.

From the time of the war period, the most useful weapon was the spear.
In the battlefield to defeat your enemy was a great deed. If the warrior had a spear it was a sign that he was a top-class samurai; that was the most important achievement in battle. The second-most important was to fight hand to hand with jujutsu techniques and pin your enemy down and bring him back alive—both these ways were the most honorable ways of fighting.

Therefore, the Hozoin-ryu used spear–against–spear techniques; to use a sword against a spear was considered foolish and dishonorable. In the battlefield a warrior who didn't hold a spear was a low-class common soldier; killing him would not bring any fame so it was better to avoid him. If there was no choice but to fight such a soldier, his body was thrown away after killing him.

Musashi was very gifted with the sword but he wasn't a high-level warrior who could wield a spear. For that reason there is doubt that he really duelled the Hozonin-ryu. If it is true he did, this would indicate that he had a very noble personality and that he had support from high-class society.

From this point the presentation of the techniques begins. First, there is an agreement that the party that strikes uses suyari and the party doing the founding techniques uses a kamayari. In each explanation here the suyari is the striking party and the kamayari is the party that executes the technique.

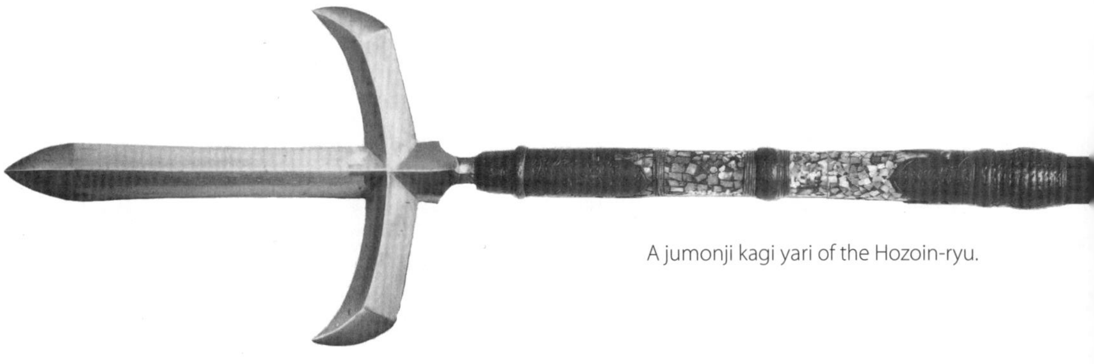

A jumonji kagi yari of the Hozoin-ryu.

Ten'yo

1

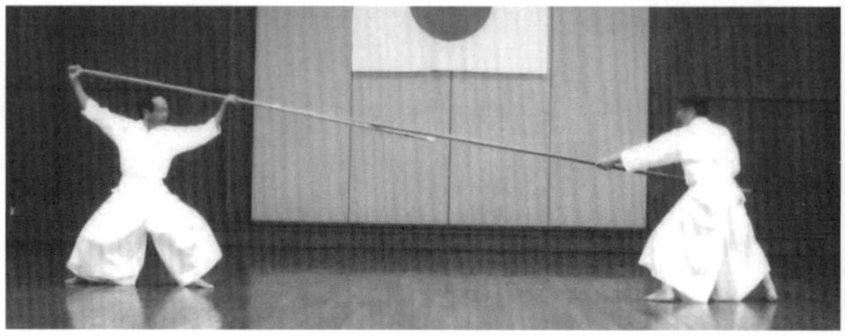

2

3

4

5

6

The suyari and the kamayari enter to the approproppriate distance, progressing to each other three steps.
Suyari is attacking the opponent's face, the kamayari lifts both of his hands and blocks, and immediately drops the suyari to the ground.
Suyari goes back to kamae and tries to stab the opponent in the thigh; kamayari lifts his right hand above the head and with his left hand blocks with the spear head.
Suyari goes back two steps, strikes the opponent's face one more time, and kamayari blocks again with the horizontal part. End of technique.
The purpose of this technique is the suyari tries to strike the face and the thigh, and the kamayari, while blocking the technique, counter-strikes and backs off. In every case, blocking the attack and counter-striking is a very difficult feat.

Ichibiki

1

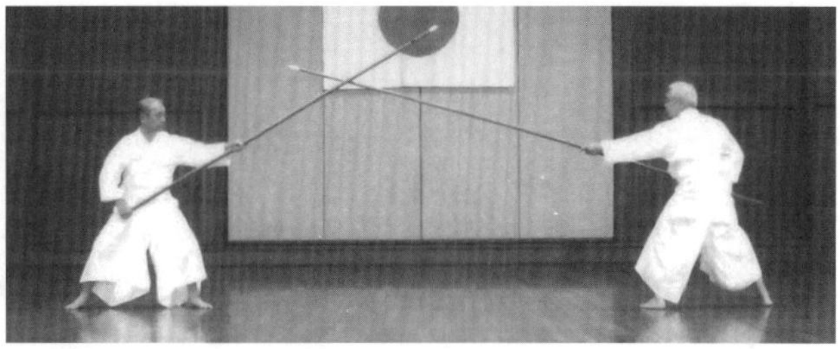

2

3

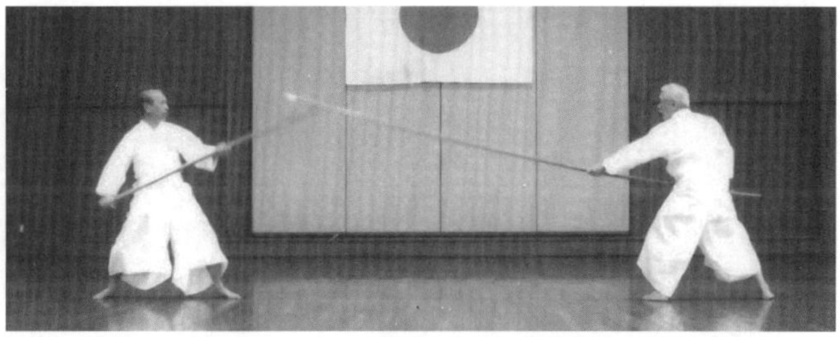

4

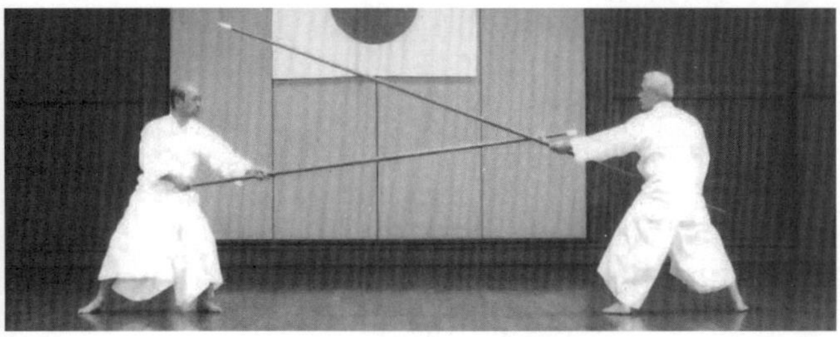

5

6

Suyari and kamayari progress toward each other three steps, and suyari strikes the face. Kamayari tilts the opponent's spear and enters to the left, immediately rotating the spear to the left and dropping the suyari to the ground. Suyari stands again and attacks the torso. Then, kamayari moves the left hand and stops suyari, and strikes from the bottom to lift suyari.
Next, while moving the right hand kamayari strikes the hands of suyari and pulls. End of technique.

Both parties pull back, and return to the base stances.
The characteristic of this technique is suyari strikes the face and the torso, kamayari first blocks to the side and then rotates and drops suyari. After that, he lifts suyari and strikes the hands with the spear head.

Egaeshi

1

2

3

4

5

6

7

8

Suyari stands in gedan, kamayari lifts both hands to Daijodan no kamae. Each takes three steps, suyari strikes the face. Kamayari blocks the hit, rotates suyari, and drops him.

Suyari stands immediately back in kamae, and fits with kamayari in jodan, then takes down kamayari to gedan, and while lifting the spears throws kamayari up.

While using the opponent's force kamayari jumps with the right leg, goes down to his knees, and strikes with the back of the spear. End of technique.

CHAPTER 3

World of Traditional Bujutsu

THE MARTIAL ARTS TRADITIONAL SYSTEM

A warrior is a person who is able to adjust to the circumstances and give a proper response fearlessly and without reluctance, regardless of the situation he is faced with. The martial arts "Bujutsu," which were created by these warriors, were techniques designed to be used in the battlefield in order to wound and kill. A theoretical, philosophical dimension to these techniques began to evolve, and became known as "Budo." Budo is a method to injure and kill the enemy; a person who trains in this art must understand death and be ready for it. One should always be thinking of how he should face his death—this is the meaning of Budo.

In the world of traditional Bujutsu, the katas have been passed on from the ryuha founders as old traditions, and through repetition of these techniques one can perfect and polish one's strength and spirit. The purpose of the practice was to have matches or duels with other schools, or to be able to deal effectively with violence or terror. It is completely different from the modern-day Budo, kendo, judo, or aikido, which have a system of rules for the matches and make physical exercise their main targets.

In the traditional Budo world there are three levels of practice known as shu-ha-ri. In the next few paragraphs I will explain the development of these levels on both the technical side and the spiritual side.

"Shu" is the task of passing on the traditional art as it was handed down by the founder of the ryuha and the successive shihan. This must be done without becoming clouded with selfish thinking or raising any doubts. The techniques must be repeated obediently, and the practitioner must be able to imitate the movements that are taught to the last detail. Once this phase is achieved the beginner stage is done and the intermediate training starts.

"Ha" is the next stage. After continuing the repetitive practice for a long time, one's character becomes refined, one's personality and unique movements and beauty emerge. Then, one begins to look and behave as his own ryuha. This is from intermediate grade to instructor grade.

"Ri" is the stage at which the practitioner continues to cultivate his spirit, and reaches a level where all wasteful movement is reduced, but he is still able to maintain the original form of the kata. He is not, however, captive to the strict form; it is a level in which it is possible to move freely from one technique to the other in order, in a way that can be used on the battlefield. This is from master class to specialist grade.

In Budo and Bujutsu, one's refined body strength and the sharpening of one's movements are measures of a high level. Furthermore, one's high spiritual level is also evidence, as are one's everyday movements carried out with elegance, of attainment of such a high level. It is important not to lose sight of the fact, however, that Budo and Bujutsu from their roots are deadly and lethal powers. Without this power the word "Bu" loses its meaning.

From these traditional forms, after years of trial and error and bloodshed, from the endless techniques that were invented, only the pure gems have been chosen, and when they are practiced their true beauty shines.

THE MOST BEAUTIFUL KAISHAKU OF BUSHIDO

"Kaishaku" is the practice of assisting someone in committing harakiri ritual suicide ("seppuku") by beheading him.

I exchanged views on this death assistance with soke Yonehara of the Sekiguchi-ryu Iai, a school which has deep knowledge about the practice. I will offer an opinion on the most beautiful seppuku and kaishaku.

As a samurai, the self-slayer is ready to die with courage out of his sense of duty. The assistant is his close friend and a trusted samurai. They have some comfortable conversation. Then the assistant, with a kind smile, and before the warrior committing ritual suicide can even acknowledge his fear of death, beheads him. By following this procedure, the suicide victim is able to peacefully enter the afterlife, without fear of death, with no resentment, with no thoughts. I think that it is the psychological state of the moment of death that matters.

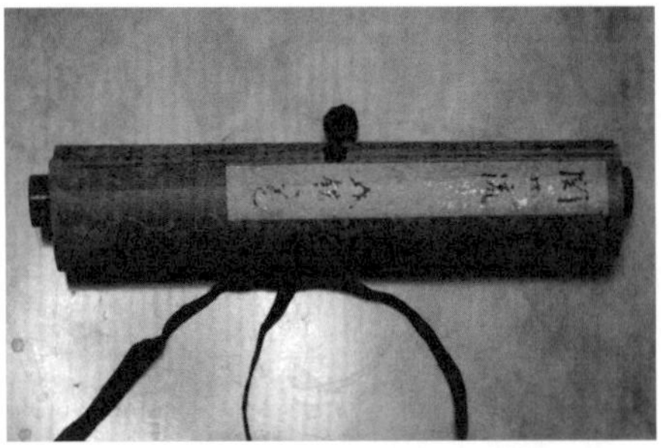

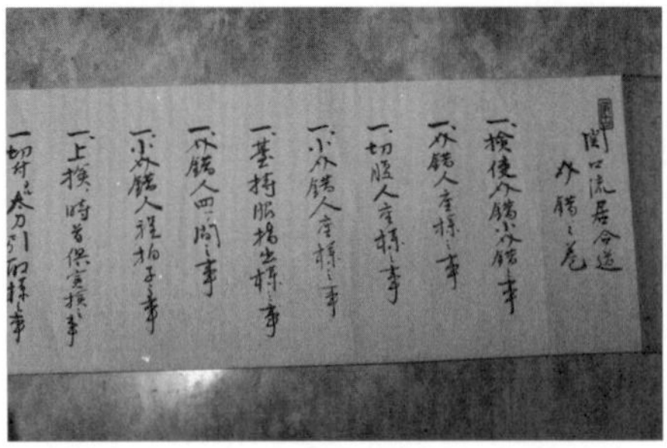

A secret makimono of Sekiguchi-ryu, which instructs the key points in assisting a hara-kiri suicide.

1

2

3

4

5

6

7

8

Pictures 1-8: The kaishaku on an emergency basis in Sekiguchi-ryu. it is important to carry out the beheading before the self-slayer experiences agony.

SWORD AGAINST ARROWS TECHNIQUES, YAKUDAKI NO JUTSU

Two thousand years ago warriors lived with their swords and were protected by them, on the battlefield or in a duel. They developed techniques which would defend them not only from other swords but also from bo, spears, arrows, and throwing weapons. The warriors held weapons with long handles like naginata, spears, and bos, and used to spin their weapons like a windmill to deflect any flying arrows or sweep throwing spears to the side. There are many tales of warriors who were extremely talented in deflecting arrows and spears on the battlefield.

Even in a case where the warrior had only his sword, he would be able to deflect arrows flying at full speed and protect his eyes by harmonizing his soul and his consciousness with this godly weapon.

The three ryuha of which I am the soke have mastered different techniques against flying weapons. First, the Kukishin-ryu's yakudai technique, and Koden Enshin-ryu's hicho technique, are techniques that make it possible to deflect high-speed arrows and throwing spears. Next, in Tenshin hyoho soden kukishin-ryu there are two techniques. The first is shidan no jutsu, and this is a technique to counter the rifle and pistol. This technique stops bullets that have already been fired from the gun, with a sword. The second is dangan-yoke. In this technique the bullet is caught in the air with a piece of fabric or cloth. Another, more religious side to the technique is a prayer that the bullet will not hit the warrior. With the same mental strength it is possible to break the enemy's sword. This technique is called setto no jutsu.

There were also ryuha that passed on techniques of deflecting arrows that had been shot, but the prior soke passed away suddenly, and these precious techniques vanished with him. At present I am the only person left who has mastered the techniques of deflecting arrows.

Even though these techniques are highly secret, in order to show to the world the difference between classic Bushido and modern Budo, I accepted the request of the English BBC television corporation and national German television, and demonstrated for the first time a combination of the Kukishin-ryu yakudai technique of facing a bow and arrow with a naginata and a bo. I also demonstrated the Koden Enshin-ryu's Hicho technique that uses a sword to face arrows and spears.

The pictures that are shown opposite are stills from the German TV show.

The key to this technique is to have full confidence in oneself and the sword. Do not be afraid of the arrow; enter a no-mind state. And do not cut the high-speed flying arrow at a sharp angle.

When cutting the arrow, if it is cut at a sharp angle the back part will lose speed and fall, but the front part can still hit the body and cause deadly injuries.

Thus, by adjusting the angle of the sword edge, one should hit or brush away the arrow without slashing it, in order to curb danger.

Picture 3: Osha no kamae — stance preparing for an arrow to be launched.
Pictures 4-6: Quickly cutting down the flying arrow.

1

2

3

4

5

6

FROM SHINKAGE-RYU TO THE NINJA SWORD TECHNIQUES OF TAISHA-RYU

Can an individual person, based on his military power, enforce rules on the rest of society? Can a whole society be controlled according to the concerns and private will of one person? Or should society be ruled by the spiritual will of the gods, or the mercy and harmony that Buddhism teaches us? Is an individual a part of the greater whole system which is known as a nation, or should his own private will and freedom have priority? These kinds of dilemmas will be a part of human society for eternity.

In the beginning until the middle of the Muromachi period (1336—1573), the feudal systems and the class divisions were still vague. The warriors had applied themselves in studies; they strove to absorb the dynastic culture of the Heian period (794—1192), and to refine their knowledge. The relation between education and sword fighting developed greatly during these times.

There was no powerful authority, however, to rule over the nation. The rules that had been decreed by the shogun and the government were not obeyed by the daimyo and the powerful families. And the internal wars between the regional leaders continued to wreak havoc on society. In this brutal world, if one individual was great enough to be remembered in the pages of history, this individual had to be one who could make a great deal of effort and also have a lot of luck. This person had to have the talent and wisdom to be able to change a known concept and adjust it to the needs of the hour. Such individuals who overcame suffering and opened the boundaries to new paths of the sword included the founder of Shinkage-ryu, Kamiizumi Ise no kami Nobutsuna, and his students, Yagyu Sekishusai Muneyoshi and Marume Kurando no Suke. In their early years Kamiizumi Ise no kami Nobutsuna and Yagyu Sekishusai had participated in many battles; they had experienced many times the hardship of losing in battle and the risk of losing their lives.

When the head of his family clan had fallen, Ise no kami had given up on his career as a general, and adopted the free lifestyle of a ronin. He became a top-class swordsman, and by founding the Shinkage-ryu he had secured his legacy and ensured his name would be remembered in the pages of history.

Yagyu Sekishusai had realized that his life was not blessed with good luck. Sekishuhsai had added to his name the Chinese characters of "boat" and "stone," endowing himself with the metaphor of a boat made of stone that cannot float on water. By doing so he had released himself from his fate of going to battle and

Image of Marume Kurando.

The banner of Ryusenkan, the Taisha-ryu dojo.

became free. As a result, his grandchildren had prospered and raised the fame of the Yagyu clan. He himself mastered the Shinkage-ryu, and the Yagyu family passed on the Shrinkage-ryu; his name is honored until this day.

Marume Kurando's formal name was Kuranosuke (this is a rank which is parallel to a vice minister). While Kurando was his rank, his real name was Nagayoshi, but he called himself Tessai. In his early years he also had suffered, though his suffering was different from that of Ise no kami and Yagyu Sekishusai's. Marume Kurando's feudal lord, Sagara, was in those days a very powerful daimyo. He controlled vast parts of what is known today as Kumamoto prefecture. Kurando served as a general in his armies. Kurando was born in Yatsushiro in the 9th year of the Tenmon Period (1540). His father was Yamamoto Yosoemon no Jou, and his mother was the princess of the Akaike Castle lord. He was the eldest son. It is said that Kurando had led his

The tomb of Marume Kurando.

Scrolls of tradition.

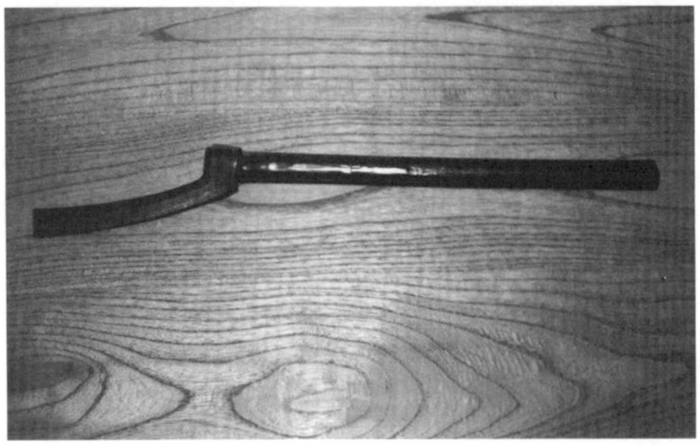

The axe of Marume Kurando.

Marume Kurando's beloved kettle for the tea ceremony.

first campaign at the age of sixteen, and due to his excellence in battle, his lord Sagara Yoshihi gave permission to bear the family name Marume as a sign of his gratitude.

These glorious days didn't last for long. When Kurando became twenty in 1559, two of the chief retainers, Higashi Nagae and Marume Yoriyoshi, began feuding with each other. As a result the Sagara clan was divided in two, and a war started. The Marume family lost the war, they were declared traitors, and were pursued. Those who were captured were killed as a part of the plan to exterminate the Marume clan.

Before the pursuit started, Kurando had depended on Amakusa Izu no kami Shigehisa. He stayed in Amakusa for two years, and before the enemy forces could reach him in 1560, he escaped to Kyoto on the advice of Ito No kami. When he arrived in Kyoto, he entered the Shikage-ryu and became a student of Kamiizumi Ise no kami. Around that time he was introduced to one of Ise no kami's best students, Anazawa Joken. It is said that he became in that period a guard in the Kyoto palace, and this is where he received his rank of Kurando no suke.

Around the year 1564, after four years of hard training in the Shinkage-ryu, he became one of its four best students, on the same level with other students such as Yagyu Sekishusai and Hikita Bungoro. In that year, Kamiizumi Ise no kami demonstrated in front of the shogun Ashikaga Yoshiteru the Shinkage-ryu kenjutsu techniques. Marume was the partner of his teacher in this demonstration as an uchidachi. The shogun was so impressed with Marume's skill that he gave him the honored title "National Treasure."

After another four years of hard training, in 1568 Marume received a full license from his teacher. Then he decided to return to his hometown, Hitoyoshi, in Higo. He still bore a grudge from the days his family was chased down by the Sagara clan, but he returned to his hometown with the high rank of Kurando no suke. He had a full licence from the famous Shikage-ryu, and had been recognized as a national treasure by the shogun. Thus he let bygones be bygones, and joined the Sagara clan as an instructor of martial arts.

During the time that Marume was back in his home town, his teacher Kamiizumi Ise no kami relied on his students to spread the ryuha: Marume Kurando

Sensei Yamakita and Mr. Sennosuke Marume, a descendant of Marume Kurando.

Sensei Yamakita and the author.

in the east of the country, and the Yagyu clan in the west. There was a time when Marume and Yagyu were renowned as the best swordsmen of the east and west respectively. When Yagyu became the kenjutsu teacher of the Tokugawa shogunate, all the daimyos around Japan started to learn the Shinkage-ryu from Yagyu. Soon after Marume came back to his hometown, Denrinbo Raikei, who would become one of his most excellent students, entered his school. This student made a big change to Kurando's techniques.

Denrinbo Raikei was a member of a Chinese pirate group that was based in Taiwan. He aspired to revive the Ming government in China. He was a member of the Watonai family, and he requested military aid from the Tokugawa government. It is said that he had studied Japanese mountain religion, he had access to information from all over the country as a yamabushi (mountain warrior), and he was familiar with ninja martial techniques. Furthermore, he had had experience of battle as a pirate.

One of Taisha-ryu's students, Higashi Shinnojou, had a duel with Togochui from the Jigen-ryu (a ryuha introduced in this book), by the order of a feudal lord. Higashi Shinnojou lost that duel. This is partly what inspired Kurando to develop secret techniques in order to defeat Jigen-ryu. He created two-sword techniques, although it is said that these secret techniques were never used. These techniques were based on throwing one of the katanas at the opponent. Because Kurando was left-handed, the short sword was held in the right hand and the long one in the left hand. Kurando learned Denrinbo's knowledge of Asian pirate fighting, ninja, and yamabushi techniques. He also practiced esoteric Buddhism. It is said that after practicing the secret methods of Marici, the Buddhist goddess, he attained enlightenment, and mastery of the techniques, which became the inner secret techniques of Taisha-ryu.

It is believed that Taisha-ryu was founded in 1587. In the eight years that Kurando lived in Kyoto he studied the inner secrets of twenty-one other ryuhas. Because he was a gifted martial artist, when he founded Taisha-ryu, he based it on kenjutsu techniques but he also included yari, naginata, iaijutsu, shuriken, and ninjutsu. Even though he founded a new ryuha, he didn't strictly develop new forms, but based his ryuha on the teaching of his mentor Kamiizumi Ise no kami's

Shinkage-ryu. Kurando said that the base of the inner secrets of the Taisha-ryu came after his practice of the Marici.

Denrinbo, as a pirate, had his hand also in international trade. While staying in Japan he studied the ninja techniques, and had access to information through his mountain warriors and ninja associates. With his help Kurando had developed his own ninpo (ninja techniques) and gathered ninja and mountain warriors from outside of Kyushu, and founded a secret organization called the Sagara ningun.

In the Edo period, the power of the great daimyo Sagara shrunk, as he controlled only a small region deep in the mountains. But because of his loyalty to the Tokugawa government, the Sagara ningun were put in charge of policing the illegal sea trade; they also took the role of protecting the Tokugawa government by keeping an eye on the resistance.

At the same time, the Yagyu family was acting as if it were the only true base of the Shinkage-ryu, and claimed the reputation of a famous ryuha. Kurando did not bother with this. He claimed that, "although Yagyu has power in the front, if there is any illegal action, Marume will supervise at the back." The actual power was in the hands of the person who was in charge of the Edo Castle secret police. The organization that gathered the ninjas Iga and Koga from the Yagyu clan was Marume's.

Kamae of Taisha-ryu Kenpo

Niju taisha sai–no-migi tenjo–no-kamae.

Niju taisha sai-no-migi tenchu-no-kamae.

Otsu-i-jin-tsuchi-no-kamae.

Shishi-no-horairi tsuchi-no-kamae.

Koui ten zujo-no-kamae.

Chukan jo-no-kamae.

Migi kodan hi-no-kame.

Migi hira-seikan-no-kamae.

Migi dokan-no-kamae.

Hidari kodan-ten-hi-no-kamae.

Shuketsu no kata of Taisha-ryu Kempo

This school is said to begin with this kata and end with this kata. A Taisha-ryu trainee starts his training with the posture "migi-hankai" by stepping his right foot forward, and ends his training with the posture "hidari-hankai" by stepping his left foot forward.

He should learn sharp oblique cutting techniques, and the base of footwork, distancing, and breathing from this kata.

1

2

3

4

5

6

7

8

9

10

11

12

13

14

15

16

The explanation of the kata

Uchidachi (assailant) and shidachi (counter-attacker) step closer to each other and put their wooden swords on the floor.
They bow towards the gods.
Then, they face each other, lift their hakama hems, and perform a rei to each other with their swords on the left waist.
They both assume Chudan no kamae, quickly hit the opponent's sword two to three times, and return to Chudan no kamae.

Ono'ono En-en-no-tachi

1

2

3

4

5

6

7

8

The explanation of the kata

In the middle of fighting, shidachi receives uchidachi's sword with his own sword sustaining with his left hand.

Then, uchidachi immediately tries to sweep-cut the counter-attacker's left leg, so shidachi strides over the sword by lifting his left leg high, and hits the assailant's two forearms from In no kamae.

Yosha-no-kata

1

2

3

4

5

6

7

8

9

10

11

12

13

14

The explanation of the kata

Both the opponents start this kata with Chudan tsune no kamae, rushing to each other with Hasso in no kamae, and harshly trying to hit each other from left and right.

Uchidachi quickly tries to sweep-cut shidachi's leg, so shidachi jumps over the sword and hits it from above, and thrusts at the assailant's throat.

Tobaku-no-kata

1

2

3

4

5

6

7

8

9

10

11

12

13

14

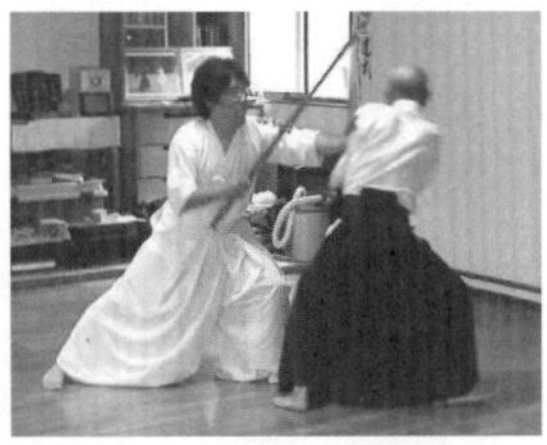
15

16

17

18

19

20

The explanation of the kata

Uchidachi assumes Hidari kodan hi no kamae, and shidachi assumes Hidari momo gamae.

Uchidachi rushes toward his opponent and executes an oblique cut from his left. Shidachi stops the sword with his left hand on the back of his sword, and winds up the assailant's sword with his own.

Shidachi shoves uchidachi away with his left hand lest the assailant should slash his legs.

Then shidachi assumes Migi kodan hi no kamae.

Uchidachi jumps far back in case his opponent should cut him.

Seihen

1

2

3

4

5

6

7

8

9

10

11

12

13

14

The explanation of the kata

Both uchidachi and shidachi assume Hidari kodan hi no kamae.

They run to each other and try to slash each other from the left and right, then they step back and assume Hira seikan no kamae.

Uchidachi tries to give a horizontal cut to the torso of shidachi.

Shidachi stops the opponent's sword, putting the tip of his sword between the assailant's right hand and the handle, and turns him backwards.

Uchidachi assumes Migi in no kamae.

Taisho (kata of kodachi)

1

2

3

4

5

6

7

8

The explanation of the kata

Uchidachi assumes batto no kame, and shidachi assumes chudan tsune no kamae with his short sword.
They rush to each other.
Shidachi suppresses uchidachi's right hand, and sticks his fingertips in the opponent's eye.

TENJIN SHIN'YO-RYU JUJUTSU HISTORY AND CHARACTERISTICS

This style was developed by a warrior named Iso Mataemon (1786-1863). This ryuha specialized in jujutsu teaching methods. Iso started to learn Yoshin-ryu at the age of fifteen, received his full license in 1801, then continued his studies in the Shinno shinto-ryu jujtsu for another six years. After he received his license, during his thirties he embarked on a musha shugyu (travelling in order to study). One day during his travels he came across a pack of about one hundred hooligans and had to fight them. In this battle he came to understand that by combining both of the styles he had learned, he could have beaten all of these people. By combining the jujutsu techniques of Yoshin-ryu and Shinno shinto-ryu he created Tenjin shin'yo-ryu. Iso Mataemon became a subject of the Tokugawa shogunate. This ryuha has had many followers, and it has been passed on until today.

It is well known that the founder of judo, Kano Jigoro, after studying this style, developed Kodokan judo based on the traditional jujutsu.

The 7th soke of Tenjin shinyo-ryu, Koichi Shibata Shihan.

Tobichigai

1

2

3

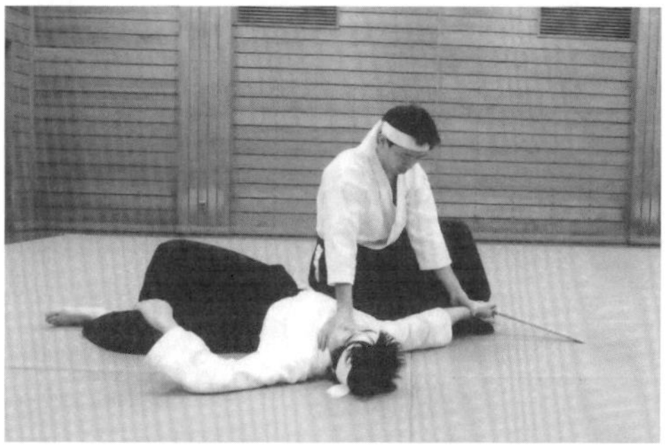

4

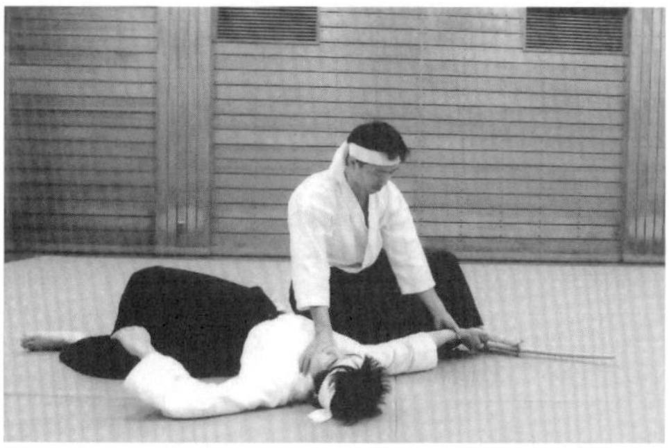

5

6

7

8

The most basic knife-grabbing technique, party A attacks with a knife from above, party B grabs his wrist and neck and pushes.

Ushiro tori

1

2

3

4

5

6

7

8

Party A grabs from the back with both hands, immediately party B hits his face with the back of his head and throws him to the front.

Koshitsuke

1

2

3

4

5

6

7

8

9

10

Party B attacks with a fist to the face, party A drops him to the back and in the instant of standing locks his neck.

ASAYAMA ICHIDEN-RYU TAIJUTSU

This style was developed in 1630–40 by Asayama Sangoro Ichidensai. Asayama studied the Shinkage-ryu, Yoshiyo kenpo, and the Kageyama shinto-ryu, then he made a ryuha that included kenjutsu, iai, bojitsu, and taijutsu (jujutsu). Asayama Ichidensai was born in 1609, and lived at the same time as the warriors Miyamoto Musashi and Sasaki Kojiro. It is said that there might have been an occasion when Asayama met Musashi and on another occasion Kojiro in Kyoto.

These days only the bujutsu and the taijutsu techniques remain. The 15th soke, Naganuma Yoshiyuki, and the 15th shike, Kaminaga Sigemi, are passing on the techniques correctly and diligently, and I am a soke dairi (representive soke) of this ryuha.

It is said that this ryuha is the root of Daito-ryu and aikido. When the samurai period ended and the Meiji period began (1868), the founder of Daito-ryu, Takeda Soukaku, studied the Asayama Ichiden-ryu, then he merged it with techniques from other ryuhas, thus giving rise to the start of Daito-ryu. In current Budo society there are a lot of rumors and stories about Daito-ryu, but none of them are clear.

In kobudo (taditional Budo), the ranks are received as scrolls (makimono), and in every scroll the lineage of that ryuha is written (from the 1st soke until the most recent soke). In the scrolls that were written by Takeda Sokaku's son, Takeda Tokimune, there was a very big difference in the lineage that was recorded in the scrolls written by the father. Furthermore, there are no scrolls dating further back than the Meiji period. Ko-budoka and I conducted extensive research on this, but despite our efforts the only scrolls that were found go back only to recent times. Furthermore, the taijutsu techniques of Daito-ryu are very similar to the techniques of Asayama Ichiden-ryu. There is another opinion that the roots of the Daito-ryu actually lie in Ryoi shinto-ryu; in either case most of the practitioners of Daito-ryu know that this ryuha was created by Takeda Soukaku, therefore Daito-ryu is not kobudo (traditional ryuha), rather it is a modern Budo.

When I went abroad I came across aikido practitioners who were convinced that by receiving their dan grade they became samurai or warriors, but aikido and Daito-ryu are not Bushido. Furthermore, Takeda Soukaku and aikido's founder Ueshiba Morihei were not the descendants of a noble or wealthy family, unlike the founder of judo, Kano Jigoro.

The last war in which a warrior held a sword and fought was the Seinan War in 1878. From that point on the era of the samurai was over, and walking in the street with a sword was strictly prohibited. This rule continues until this day. In the wake of the wars that were waged by the old-style warriors, there rose many modern martial arts: judo, kendo, karate, aikido, and modern naginata. All these arts have effectively removed the samurai class characteristics and have become physical exercises to improve health. However, even after founding Kodokan judo, most of Kano Jigoro's students learned the taijutsu techniques of the Ichiden-ryu, which differ from judo. If not carried out with extreme care, these techniques can cause a broken bone or even cost a life.

15th soke Yoshiyuki Naganuma and 16th soke Shigeyoshi Kaminaga.

15th soke Yoshiyuki Naganuma.

Kasumi gaeshi

1

2

3

4

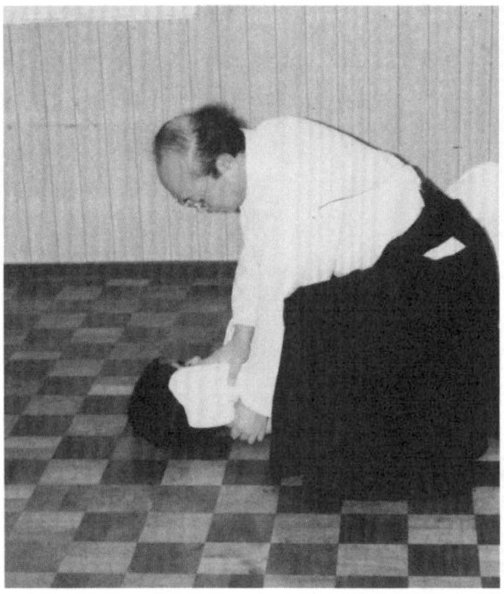

5

The enemy comes from the rear and grabs the left hand with his right and pulls. From this position, while taking a step back, lift your elbow, turn the wrist, and grab the enemy's wrist. Then, with the right hand hold the enemy below the elbow and push, grab the front arm, take a step forward with the right leg, and knock him down. Once fallen push his joint so he cannot move.

Kaeri nage

1

2

3

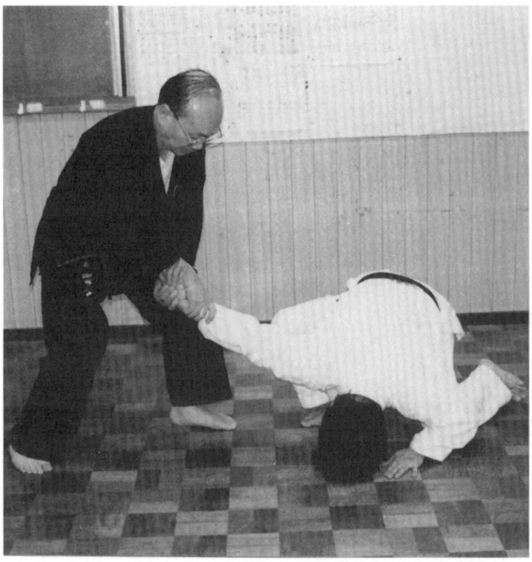

4

The enemy comes from the rear, grabs the right wrist with his right hand, and pulls. With this pulling take a step back and lower the right elbow, open your hand, and grab the enemy's hand from the little finger. At the same time with the left hand grab the enemy's back hand (picture 3), grab the enemy's right hand so his wrist cannot move, and while taking the right leg back twist his wrist.

Irichigai

1

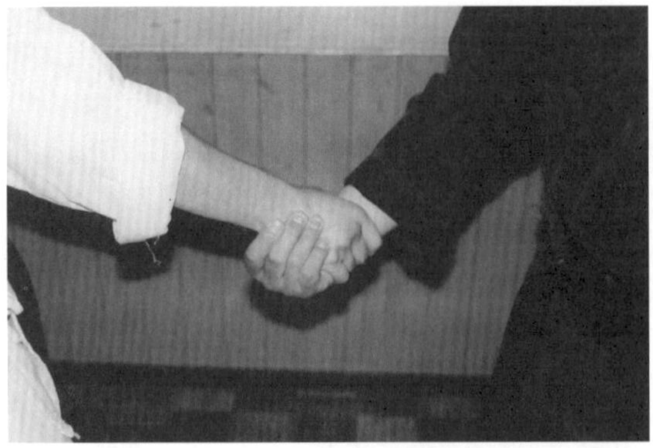

2

3

4

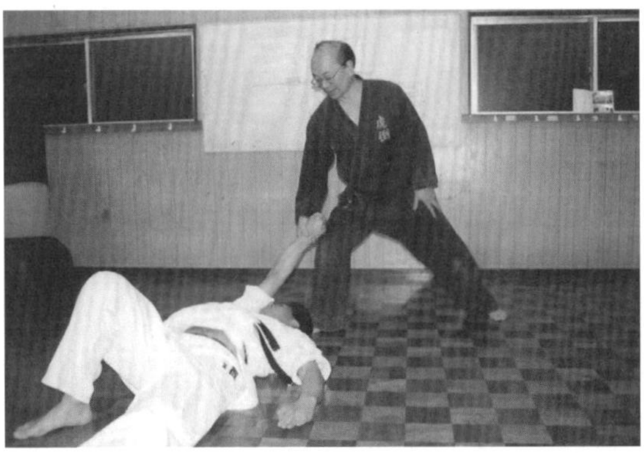

5

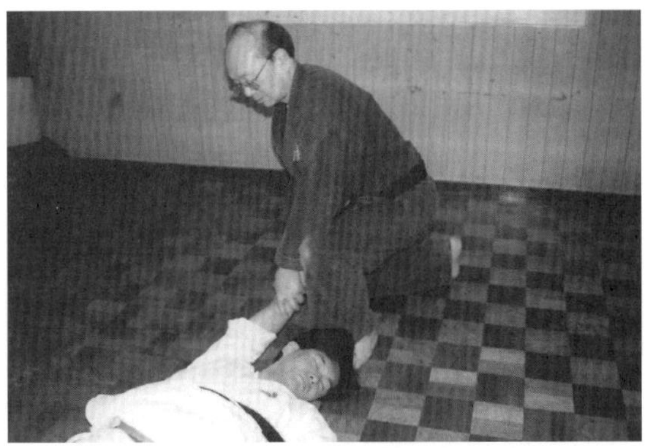

6

The enemy grabs the right hand with the right hand diagonally. Step with the right leg to the front of the enemy's body, and while holding his hand pull the right hand to your stomach. Hold so he cannot escape, and place the left hand under the enemy's arm on his lower stomach.

While stepping, open your body to the right and lean the left shoulder down and forward, and hold his wrist firmly. In order not to break a bone or get injured, the enemy should roll to the front; after rolling pin down by pushing the elbow.

Hikiotoshi

1

2

3

4

5

6

7

The enemy steps forward with the left leg and grabs the right side of the chest. Put the right hand on the left hand (Pictures 3 and 4) then step back with the right leg and pin the left hand down firmly.

TAKENOUCHI-RYU JUJUTSU (TORITE, KOSHIMAWARI)

This style was developed in the year 1532, in the land of Mimasaka, in Heiwagou (today Okayama prefecture). It was made by a general of Ichinose Castle, Takeuchi Hisamori. The son of Hisamori, Hisakatsu, continued his father's legacy and travelled throughout Japan to have real sword duels in order to polish his technique.

In 1620 he was privileged enough to have the emperor himself (Gomizunoo) watch him while he was demonstrating jujutsu techniques. Because of this occasion, Hisakatsu received from the Konoekanpaku (the equivalent these days of the Prime Minister) the rank of hitachinosuke, and the diploma of hinoshitakaizan that declared that he was Japan's preeminent martial artist (the equivalent to the emperor's honor medal today).

In addition, the son of Hisakatsu, Hisayoshi, received the rank of kaganosuke and the hinoshitakaizan diploma in 1663. It was the first time in Japan's history that a father and son had received recognition from the government for being top-class budoka.

In three generations, the Takenouchi-ryu, which used jujutsu techniques as its base, had grown into a famous school throughout Japan. Many of the nation's warriors have studied this ryuha, and it has been spread and passed down through the generations for 479 years until this day. Moreover, this ryuha has influenced many of the jujutsu schools that came after it. It is considered in Okayama prefecture as an intangible cultural asset, and the offspring of the founder Hisamori Takenouchi are still keeping the tradition and the techniques.

The Takenouchi-ryu mainly focusses on full armor techniques which are to be used on the battlefield, but it also practices kenjutsu, yari, naginata, bo, fist techniques, and arresting techniques which are essential in jujtsu. In particular, con-

1

2

3

4

5

6

7

8

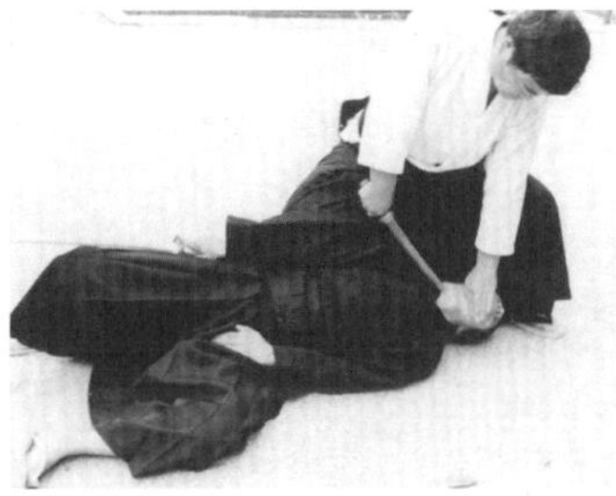

9

10

cerning the koshimawari, small weapons techniques, it is said that when Hisamori went to the mountains to practice kenjutsu, he practiced very rigorously and became tired so he used his bukutou as a pillow and fell asleep. Then, a white-haired mountain warrior appeared and taught him secret techniques. The bokuto that Hisamori held was 2 shaku 4 sun (72cm) and was too long for the study of these top secret techniques, making it somewhat worthless, so Hisamori cut the bokutou in half to 1 shaku 3 sun (36cm), and the warrior was able to teach him correctly. The koshimawari, small weapons secret techniques, have been preserved and passed on until this day.

In this book one technique from the koshimawari techniques known as the nakasaide technique will be demonstrated by Takenouchi Takeo Shihan and Kamizaki Shihan.

1) From the nakasaide, tachi-otoshi

Party B holds a sword and stands in jodan, party A holds a short sword (kodachi), puts it on the level of the hip, and waits. When party B attacks from above party A takes one step forward with his left leg and strikes with the kodachi on party B's wrist. Then he enters to the right side and grabs his chin and pulls it to the left, while holding the chin firmly, he stabs party B in the throat. This technique is also effective when wearing full armor; it is easy to notice the feature of the koshimawari techniques of Takenouchi-ryu.

KASHIMA SHINTO-RYU KENJUTSU

This style is the very root of Japanese kenjutsu; this cultural asset was passed on for 1,600 years and still exists today. In the year 414, before the katana was born and people still used tsuruga to fight, there was a Shinto priest named Kuninazu no Mahito in the kashima shrine. In order to reveal the inner secrets of the kenjutsu, he built an altar on the shrine grounds, and risked his life to practice neto, a special prayer to the strongest war god Takemikazuchi. This extremely strong shamanistic prayer is continued for 1,000 days, and by immersing himself in this prayer he received the practical and spiritual basic teaching of kenjutsu from this god.

These are the features of old Japanese Shinto:

1) The power that is born by believing in a god (shinryoku).
2) The power that is born by praying to a god (kitoryoku).
3) The power that is born by action (koryoku).
4) The spiritual power of holding a tsuruga (reiryoku).

The unification of these four powers is the basic mental state.

Furthermore, the fighting method is an ever changing form, and Kuninazu no Mahito was the first who succeeded in transforming this art into a fixed kata. Then, from the fixed kata he extracted techniques, found the logic behind them, and discovered their basic principles. The kenjutsu kata that Kuninazu no Mahito had made after this style was called the kashima no tachi, and was spread widely. This ryuha is the root of most of the ryuhas in Japan.

In the 6th century, a country called Shiragi, which is old Korea, tried to invade Japan through Kyushu several times. The Japanese government, in order to respond to the situation, gathered many warriors from the north-west of the country in the Kashima Shrine, and after training in long sword kenjutsu, they were assigned as guards in Kyushu. Because of the guards' good work, Shiragi abandoned the invasion. Then the warriors that were proceeding to Kyushu spread the name of kashima no tachi, and from all over Japan many people came to study this kenjutsu.

The result was that the kenjutsu and other fighting arts are said to have started from the west of Japan, and that the kashima sword techniques are the roots of Japanese kenjutsu. This ryuha's history is very long; from Kuninazu no Mahito to the Urabe clan, this ryuha had been passed on by the same clan for 1,600 years.

Bronze statue of Takemikazuchi no Mikoto.

Portrait of Tsukahara Bokuden.

The great torii entrance of Kashima Jingu Shrine.

The inside of the dojo.

Soke Tsunetaka Yoshikawa.

Kashima Jingu Shrine.

The entrance of the house of the Yoshikawas.

The on-site dojo in the grounds of the house.

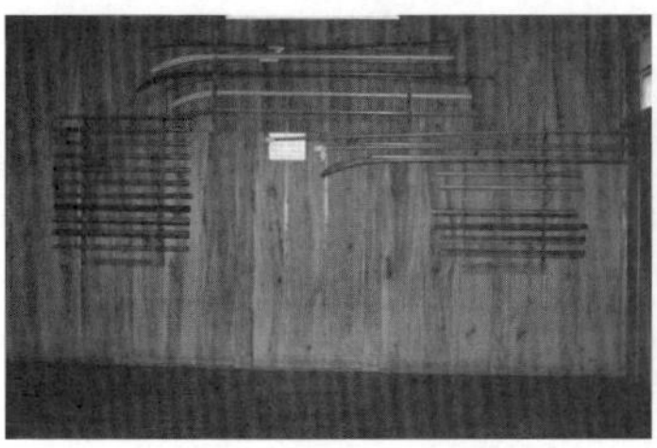

The wall of the dojo.

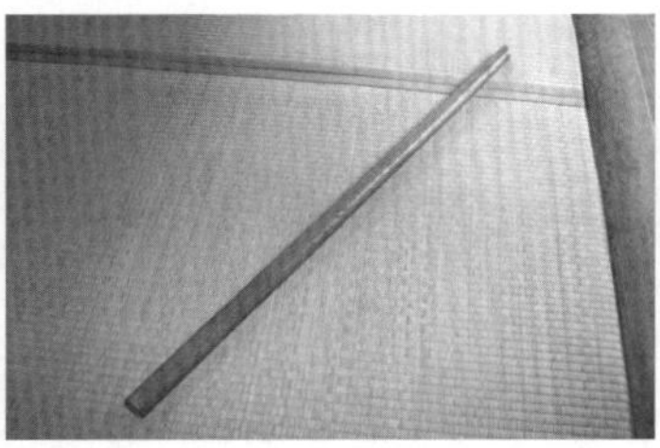

Bokuto (wooden sword).

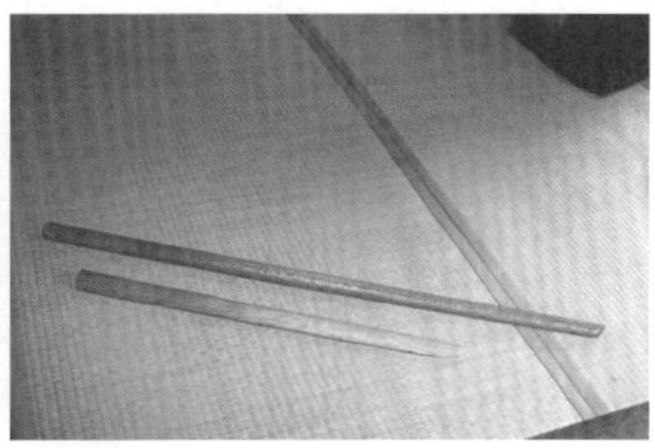

Bokutos.

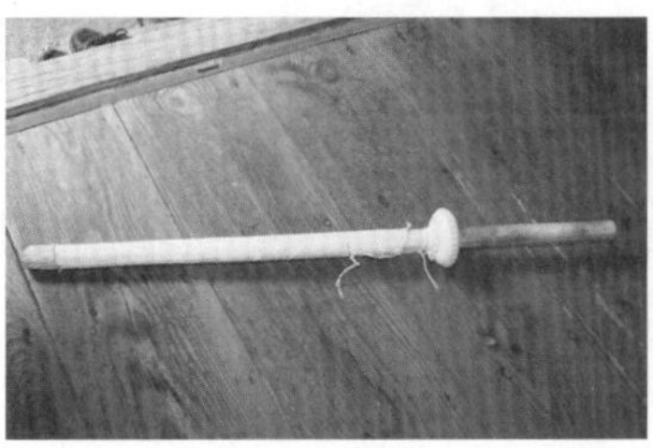

Fukuro shinai (bamboo sword covered with leather).

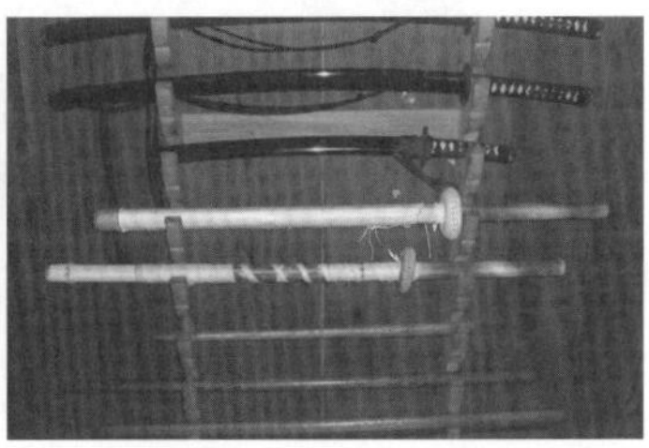

Sword rack.

These days, of the descendants of the Urabe clan, Mr. Tsunetaka Yoshikawa is the current soke. This ryuha is divided into three traditional parts. The first two are from the 5th century to the 10th century, the oldest style (tsurugi kenjutsu). The middle-aged style dates from the 11th century until the 15th century (katana kenjutsu). The latest style is from 1489.

One member of the Urabe clan, named Tusukahara Bokuden, was a genius swordsman, and during his life he had sixty duels without losing even one. At some point in his life he taught the shogun Ashikaga, and by doing that he gained the title of the best swordsman in Japan. As a high-class warrior he always rode a horse, and, followed by more then sixty disciples, he toured Japan teaching kenjutsu. In Japan's kenjutsu history he has a legendary status. In addition, Bokuden had added many new kenjutsu techniques, and also many new spiritual and mental concepts, and new ways of dealing with various situations. He changed the named of these ryuha to Kashima shinto-ryu. The specialities of this ryuha are techniques with full armor and helmets.

1

2

3

4

5

6

Pictures 1-4: Saluting to Sihan Yasusada Okami.
Pictures 5-6: Allowed to join the trainees.

1 Tachii.

2 Seigan.

3 Seigan (from the side).

4 Jodan.

5 Jodan (from the side).

6 Sha no kamae.

7 In no kamae.

8 In no kamae (from the side).

9 Hara tombo.

10 Koshi tombo.

11 Koshi tombo (from the side).

12 Yume no makura.

Migi hotsu no kamae to kiri otoshi

1

2

3

4

Carrying the sword on the right shoulder, Migi hotsu no kamae, then cutting diagonally; this kata is a typical armor technique.

Enzan no tachi

Picture 1: pointing the sword to a faraway mountain, Enzan no kamae.
Pictures 3-6: Uchidachi attacks straight, shitachi captures the sword, then lifts the opponent's sword and quickly kneels on his right knee, stabbing the throat. End of technique.
It is worth pointing out that this technique was presented in Shinto Muso-ryu, and is the model of a technique called suigetsu; with that technique Muso Gonnosuke beat Musashi's two-sword techniques.

1

2

3

4

5

6

Ichi no tachi – This technique is about 450 years old.

1

2

3

4

5

6

7

8

9

10

11

Right side uchidachi, left side shitachi.
Both sides stand in aiseigan no kamae and progress towards each other. Uchidachi changes to Hasso no kamae and attacks in order to knock shitachi's sword down. Shitachi takes a step left and stands in jodan no kamae, and instantly blocks the strike. Then again uchidachi is going to strike so, with the left leg, shitachi takes a step forward and strikes the wrist. End of technique.

Nanatsu no aisute no tachi

1

2

3

4

5

6

7

8

9

0

11

12

First, both sides strike, after the strike both sides stand in sha no kamae, then shitachi takes off uchidachi's attack by a right to left counter strike. This is a kata that helps to learn rhythm and timing.

13

14

15

16

17

18

19

20

21

22

23

24

I no tachi

1

2

3

4

5

6

7

8

9

10

11

Uchidachi on the right side attacks straight, at that time shitachi defends himself by hiding behind his sword while the blade is faced down, and steps to the left. Then, he cuts the opponent's left side of the neck. End of technique.

Aigasumi (unjo no tomoe)

– With special permission from Okami Shihan, the author took part in this technique.

1

2

3

4

5

6

7

8

9

10

On the right side the author as shitachi, on the left side Okami Shihan as uchidachi.

Both sides stand in Aiseigan no kamae, advancing towards each other. Both change to jodan and strike straight, but shitachi's sword knocks down uchidachi's sword.

When uchidachi returns to Chudan no kamae, shitachi moves to Jodan no kamae. Without giving an opening he knocks down uchidachi's sword while uchidachi is trying to stab. End of technique.

JIGEN-RYU KENJUTSU

Jigen-ryu was completed around 1590, in a place called Satsuma (today Kagoshima), by Togo Chui, whose formal name was Togo Hizen no kami Tobei Shigekata. The roots of the Jigen-ryu come from the Tenshinsho Jiken-ryu, and its third shihan was Iizasa Wakasa no kami. His disciple, Tose Yozaemon, went to Kashima Shrine, and while offering prayers to the gods and practicing very hard, he received a revelation of secret techniques and became able to strike down a flying swallow. Then, he founded the Tenshinsho Jiken-ryu.

One of the "grandchild disciples" of Yozaemon, a person called Akasaka Yakuro, learned kenjutsu from a second generation disciple called Kaneko Shinnkuro, and avenged his father's death. Only warriors were officially permitted to conduct this kind of revenge. However, filled with regret for taking a life, he changed his name to Zenkichi and became a priest. In his later days he lived in Kyoto, and served as the head priest of the Tenneiji temple.

In 1587, Togo Chui came with his master to Kyoto, and by the orders of his master he started to study lacquer craftsmanship, and the craft of making tsubas. During the same period he applied himself to zen meditation in the Tenneiji temple. One day, Togo Chui heard from a zen master that Zenkichi Osho was a master swordsman who had avenged his father's death. After hearing, this he watched Zenkichi cleaning the garden. When he had finished tidying up, Zenkichi held the broom diagonally in a kamae, and recited a poem.

The figure of Zenkichi in kamae, with his readiness and determination, was truly impressive. Therefore, Chui asked to be introduced to him and to become his disciple. But because Zenkichi was a Buddhist priest, he could not teach fighting techniques.

However, Chui did not give up and for sixty days he continued pleading to Zenkichi to become his disciple, and in the end he agreed. From that day on, every evening he received very strict guidance, and after six months of training, he managed to learn from Zenkichi all the secrets, and returned to Satsuma.

Togo Chui first studied Taisha-ryu, but since the trip to Kyoto in 1588 he maintained the teachings of Zenkichi Osho. In his own house he used a wooden stick and stroked a tree every morning 3,000 times and every evening 8,000 times, for 1,000 days. Because of this special way of training, and the spiritual teachings that have been added, the techniques created by Zenkichi and the Jigen-ryu were different. The style that is passed on today is a new Jigen-ryu kenjutsu style.

Togo Chui's kenjutsu gained a sound reputation, and the lord of Shimazu heard about it, and ordered him to duel with the fencing master of the feudal clan "Han," the Taisha-ryu instructor Azuma Shinnojo. Because it was impossible to refuse the orders of one's master he had no choice but to fight. When they fought Chui broke Azuma Shinnojo's boken in two and won the duel, whereupon he was ordered to become the fencing instructor of the clan.

Togo Chui had fought more than forty-six duels with warriors from top-class ryuha and never lost, and everybody he defeated became his diciple. Moreover, Togo Chui had refused to fight with many famous warriors: Miyamoto Musashi, Yagyu Munenori, Marume Kurando, Izumi Ise no kami, among others. He was, however, sent more than nineteen times to execute "joiuchi." Joiuchi was the practice of tracking down warriors who had violated the law or broken an important rule, and rather than performing their ritual duty of seppuku, as they had been ordered to do, had instead resisted violently or run away. The joiuchi demanded the errant warrior be caught and beheaded as an official punishment. It was a job for one man. But, in these cases, the disgraced warrior was often desperate to protect his life, so this kind of fight was a lot more dangerous then a standard duel with a warrior.

Miyamoto Musashi was well known not only for his fighting skills but also for practicing sumie painting, crafting tsuba for swords, and crafting small shurikens, all of the highest quality. Togo Chui had also made very fine lacquer crafts and tsubas, and he also founded Jigen-ryu, recognized as one of Satsuma province's (now Kagoshima prefecture's) great cultural assets. Looking at all his legacy and crafts, one can see that he had a truly extraordinary talent.

Zenkichi Osho.

Togo Chui in sokutai (a kimono worn by court nobles).

The makimonos transmitted from Zenkichi Osho to Togo Chui.

The gold-relief lacquered bowls made by Togo Chui.

A tsuba made by Togo Chui.

A guide of Jigen-ryu hyoho-syo (dojo).

Master Shigenori Togo, the 12th soke.

Saluting Soke Shigenori Togo.

The on-site dojo in the house of the Togos.

Branches of an isu tree (citrus family) used as wooden swords for usual training.

Bowing to wooden swords when one starts and finishes training.

The Feature of Jigen-ryu:

Jigen-ryu has many techniques but, before starting the kata practice, one has to conduct the tree-striking practice 3,000 times in the morning and 8,000 times in the evening. This means the study starts and ends with tree striking; this simple left-right striking is the inner secret. If one fights, one has to be in the state of mind that either he will kill or be killed. These are the only two options, this is the way the ryuha has been taught for many years.

As a rule, private fights are admonishments; in order to keep that rule the swords' tsuba and saya were tied up together with a wire. If one was faced with no choice but to fight, the fight must end in one blow—the warrior must strike the opponent only once. The readiness for death was at its extreme—there must be no doubt with the single strike; a second strike was considered failure.

At the end of the samurai period (1863-1888) many of the warriors who made the revolution for modern Japan (Meiji Restoration) studied the Jigen-ryu, and they fought with the Tokugawa government as revolutionary armies. At that time, the fighting was so violent that it is said that if one could avoid the first strike there is a chance for winning.

Togo soke instructs the author in Jigen-ryu kenpo.

The basics of Jigen-ryu kenjutsu.

Tachiki-uchi (hitting a wide wooden target).

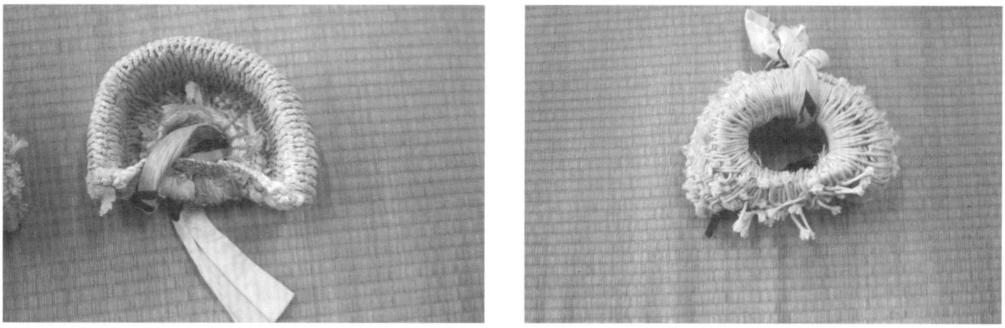

A tsuba for usual training, made from twisted pieces of paper.

1

2

3

Setting a tsuba onto a wooden sword.

Stances of Jigen-ryu kenjutsu.

Oki Tombo.

Oki Tombo (from the side).

Tombo no kamae.

Gyaku (reverse) Tombo.

Sha no kamae.

Receiving instructions on how to use the naga-bokut

1

2

3

4

5

6

7

8

9

10

The use of the long wooden sword (naga-bokuto), straight cut, side cut, stab.

1

2

The way of holding the long wooden sword.

Naga-bokuto vs. tachi

1

2

3

4

5

6

7

Pictures 1-6: The naga-bokuto stands in Tonbo no kamae and strikes. Pictures 7-10: The daito manages to stab and knock the naga-bokuto down, and stabs.

8

9

10

Kodachi

A-1

A-2

B-1

B-2

A. From Okitonbo no kamae the kodachi moves, and before moving the daito, strikes the wrist.

B. Pushing the daito's strike down and going to strike the face, then changing to Tombo no kamae, and again pushing down the striking enemy, changing to a final attack.

C-1

C-2

1

2

3

4

The specialty of an attack from Sha no kamae is that the center is in the heels.

Receiving instruction in the use of a small sword (kodachi). The kodachi was learned by the ladies of the lord. There were two initiations for this weapon, which was learned by many women. When the lord had to go to battle, in order to protect the castle they were required to know the techniques of kodachi and naginata.

1

2

3

Strike from Sha no kamae, the enemy on the right side stands in Tonbo no kamae, the other side in sha no kame; the practice is to knock the enemy's strikes to the left.

1

2

3

4

From the form of striking the wrist, with the left hand grabbing the enemy from behind and taking him off balance, attacking the throat. End of technique. This technique is performed alone.

1

2

3

4

When this technique is done with two people, at the time the opponent strikes, take one step with the left leg to get out of the attack line, quickly enter the opponent's body side, and with the left hand turn the shoulder and unbalance your opponent, and give a fatal blow with the kodachi.

TENSHIN SHODEN KATORI SHINTO-RYU KENJUTSU

This style was founded by Iisaza Choisai Ienao, who in his early days served the shogun Ashikaga Yoshimasa. He was renowned as a great warrior. When Iisaza Choisai became sixty, he started seeking the inner secret techniques of tosojutsu (sword and spear techniques). He prayed for 1,000 days to the gods of katori.

In that retreat he performed saikai mokuyoku (praying to the gods at 2.A.M while bathing in pure water). He also practiced to the extent that his bones became like powder, and after 1,000 days it is said he received makimonos from the gods of katori.

In 1448, at the age of sixty-five, he completed the development of the ryuha. He passed away at the age of 120. Since that time, many of Japan's greatest warriors and generals have studied this ryuha, and it has influenced some of Japan's most important ryuhas, among them: Shinkage-ryu, Jiki shinkage-ryu, Taisha-ryu, and Jigen-ryu. One can say that it had great influence on the medieval period in Japan. Moreover, the tradition of this ryuha has been passed down from father to son for more then 562 years. Now, the 20th soke is Iisaza Yasusada soke. The ryuha's techniques have been handed down to Shihan Otake Risuke, and he spreads these famous ryuha's techniques to the rest of the world.

Katori Shinto-ryu was created as a battlefield full armor martial art, but it is one of Japan's most classic Bujutsu teachings. It includes various teachings and techiques of kenjutsu, iai, jujutsu, yari, naginata, bojutsu, shurikenjutsu, ninjutsu (hiding techniques), gunbaiho (controlling a battle), chikujoho (castle construction), astronomy, geography, Shinto, Buddhism, esoteric Buddhism etc. I have had the honor of receiving instructions from Shihan Otake in the iai and kenjutsu techniques.

Katori jingu Prayer Shrine.

Katori jingu Shinto Shrine.

Traditional Dojo in Iizasa-House.

Sculpture of Iizasa Choisai and his wife.

Portrait of Iizasa Choisai.

Calligraphy of Tenshin shoden.

Documents of spear against sword.

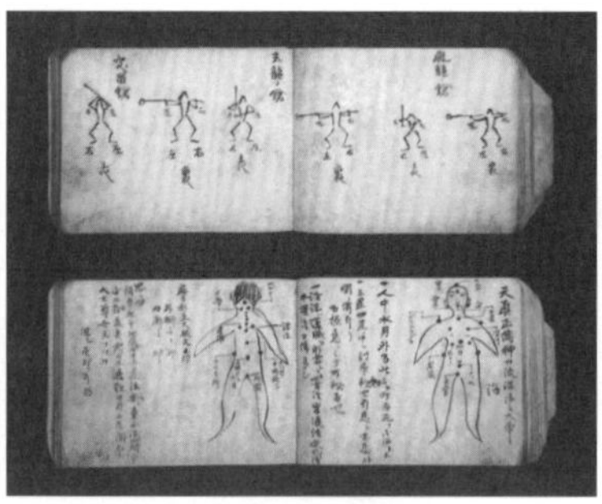

Picture of Tombo no kamae.

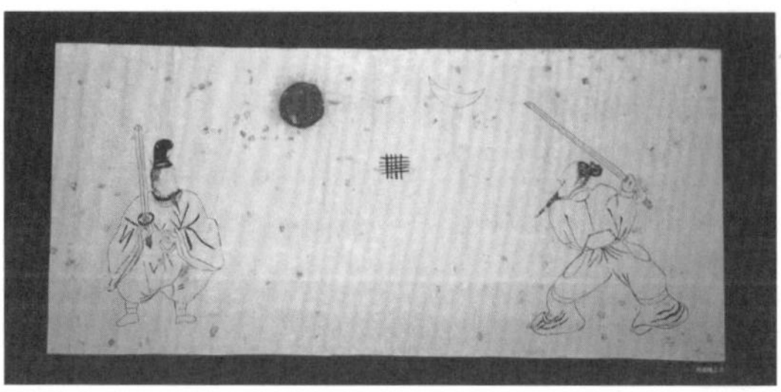

Picture of the founder and the Rising Sun.

Present Soke Yasusada Iizasa and the author.

Jinmukan dojo of Shihan Otake.

Shihan Risuke Otake.

Saluting Shihan Otake

1

2

3

4

5

6

Sihan Otake and the author.

Receiving instructions given by Shihan Otake

In order to avoid running out of breath or exhausting oneself in the battlefield, one kind of practice is to connect a number of katas together. This way of training is special to this ryuha.

Seigan no kamae (front).

Seigan no kamae (side).

Shin no kamae (front).

Shin no kamae (side).

Gedan no kamae (side).

Gedan no kamae (front).

Gyaku no gedan (front).

Gyaku no gedan (side).

Hidari Jodan (side).

Hidari Jodan (front).

Migi Jodan (front).

Migi Jodan (side).

Sha no kamae (side).

Sha no kamae (front).

In no kamae (front).

In no kamae (side).

Uketachi no kamae (side).

Uketachi no kamae (front).

Harai tachi no kamae.

Receiving instructions on Itsutsu no tachi

In this picture Shihan Otake gives instructions to the author as a beginner of this school.
On the right side Shihan Otake (eighty-four years old)
On the left side the author (sixty-four years old)

1

2

3

4

5

6

7

8

9

10

11

12

13

14

15

16

17

18

19

20

21

22

23

24

25

26

27

28

29

30

31

32

33

Explanation of the kata

Pictures 1-5: In order to start the practice both sides stand in Seigan no kamae. The author attacks the face from the side, in the last second he takes a step back and strikes the wrist. But in order that the practice could continue Shihan Otake blocks the strike as shown in picture 8. Next, in Pictures 9-12, Shihan Otake attacks the face so the author tries to cut the wrist from below.

Pictures 13-20: The author receives instructions on the position of the tip of the sword (kisaki), then Shihan Otake attacks. Again, the author holds the sword with both hands and blocks the strike, then stands up and tries to cut the torso, but Shihan Otake blocks the hit, so the author knocks the opponent's sword down and cuts the left side of the neck, pausing the practice.

Pictures 21-33: Both sides stand in Seigan no kamae. The author tries to cut the torso, and then Shihan Otake takes a step back and tries to cut the wrist, the author takes a step back, changes to Hasso no kamae, and tries again to cut the torso but then again Shihan Otake is trying to strike the wrist, so when taking the right leg back as seen in Picture 29, Shihan Otake is now trying to cut the torso. Then the author, while taking a step back with the left leg, strikes in order to block the torso strike, and Shihan Otake switches and pushes the author's sword down. Then Shihan pushes down so the author swings the sword up and tries to attack straight but, as seen in Pictures 32-33, again the strike is being blocked, so the author dives under the opponent's sword and makes a big step, then repeats the whole technique again.

Gogyo no tachi

Also in this technique the author receives instructions from Shihan Otake.

1

2

3

4

5

6

7

8

9

10

11

12

13

14

15

16

17

Explanation:

Both sides stand in Ukedachi no kamae. Shihan Otake strikes the wrist so, as seen in picture 4, the author takes a step with the right leg and, using the hilt (tsuka) to block the strike, immediately cuts the torso. Then, as seen in Picture 5, shihan is blocking the strike so the author kneels on his left knee and invites the opponent to strike. Then shihan tries to strike but as seen in Picture 7, the author blocks the strike and stands up, and pushes the opponent, hitting him with the hilt.

Iaijutsu, Yukiai gyakunuki no tachi

Iaijutsu is designed for situations when one is walking alone in the street, or inside buildings, and in situations of a surprise attack.

1

2

3

4

5

6

7

8

9

10

11

12

13

Explanation: The enemy suddenly appears from the front; he tries to cut the torso, so shihan steps back with the right leg and draws the sword upside down, with the hand grabbing from the upper side of the hilt, and cuts the right wrist of the enemy. When the enemy flinches for a moment, shihan takes another step and cuts him down.

Gyakunuki no tachi no futarigumi de sotei giho (drawing backwards, done with two people)

1

2

3

4

5

6

In this kata, the surprise attack comes from the back. When grabbed from the back, shihan takes the hilt down, hitting the enemy with the sheath (saya) in the crotch. In the second that the opponent's movement is stopped, he draws the sword and stabs.

TATSUMI-RYU KENJUTSU

In the innermost techniques of the martial arts, spiritual enlightenment is often presented as mushin (no mind) or muga no kyochi (spiritual state of perfect selflessness). It resembles the Zen Buddhist enlightenment experience. Before Buddhism was brought to Japan, the original religion was Shinto, which has a strong belief in the divine protection of the gods, and that one who prays diligently enters a state of being possessed by the gods. I am in possession of old books in which it is written that if one continues these prayers, he separates from present consciousness and the ability to remove confusion and fears awakens. He senses subtleties and the way of moving in the battlefield.

Soke Kato and his son.

There is a tale of a warrior called Tatsumi Sankiyo who, during the Warring States Period, had countless duels in which he was victorious. Despite this, he always feared for the safety of his life. In order to explore this spiritual state he made up his mind to study old Shinto. After a long time of practicing very strict prayer in the Tsumayama daimyojin shrine he reached the spiritual enlightenment of nothingness (muga no kyochi).

Soke Kato and the author.

On the battlefield he was able to sense the subtleties of attacking and counterattacking before they happened. Thus, possessing the principles to certain victory he founded the Tatsumi-ryu. This style has been instrumental in developing kenjutsu, iai, jujutsu, sojutsu (spear), and bojutsu techniques. The essence of these techniques lies in the fact that not only are they extremely powerful, they are also very educational and refined. It became a ryuha that was taught only in the region of Sakurahan, which was in Shimofusa (today Chiba prefecture), and many warriors have studied its techniques. One of the warriors who studied this ryuha was Fukuzawa Yukichi. Towards the end of the Warring States Period and the beginning of modern Japan he contributed to Japan's internationalization, and he established the Keio University. These days you can see his portrait on the 10,000 yen bill. At present the 22nd Soke Hiroshi Kato maintains the ryuha.

Kato soke and the beginner class.

The kamae of Tatsumi-ryu kenjutsu

Migi jodan.

Hidari jodan.

Kata jodan.

Hasso.

Waki gamae.

Seigan (chudan).

Gedan.

Receiving instruction of the batto (drawing)

1

2

3

4

5

6

7

In modern iaido only the form is taught, but iai is one aspect of Bushido; it is an essential part of the martial arts.
In this style, in order to protect the wrists from being cut by the opponent, the old drawing style has been taught for many years: drawing is done along the body.
Pictures 1, 2: Turn the saya in a horizontal angle and turn the blade down, and with the thumb and the pointing finger prepare to draw the sword.
Pictures 3-5: While pulling the saya draw the sword along the body. With this way of drawing the chances of the wrist being cut by the opponent are small.

Kenjutsu first technique Muko no kata

1

2

3

4

5

6

7

8

9

10

11

12

Left party is called ukekata, the right party shikata.
Pictures 1-4: Both parties stand in aiseigan, ukekata changes stance to hidari jodan and they approach each other until entering the maai. Ukekata shouts "iay-i" and shikata shouts "iee-i." This is a unique kiai of this ryuha.

Pictures 5-8: Shikata strikes from the center then shikata lifts the sword and receives the attack with the shinogi of the sword. The way that ukekata's sword was knocked out is shown in picture 6. Without giving an opening shikata attacks the front. End of technique.

Kenjutsu third technique Maeja

1

2

3

4

5

6

7

8

9

10

11

12

In these pictures ukekata is on the right side and shikata on the left.
Pictures 1-4: Both parties stand in aiseigan, then ukekata changes to Gedan no kamae, shikata changes to migi jodan. Both parties proceed towards each other until entering the maii, then ukekata shouts "iyai-i" and shikata shouts "iee-i;" this is a unique kiai of this ryuha.
Pictures 5-8: Ukekata stands in seigan no kame so shikata strikes the wrist, then ukekata, while taking a step back, tries to hit the side (yokomen). Shikata uses the sword to block the hit and uses the shinogi to receive the hit.
Picture 9: Ukekata's sword is knocked down.
Without giving an opening shikata attacks the front. End of technique.
Pictures 10–12: Both parties stand in aiseigan, and return to first stance.

Kenjutsu, receiving instruction of Muko no kata

1

2

3

4

5

6

7

8

9

10

11

The author receives direct instruction from the 22nd soke of the technique moko no kata. The right side ukekata stands in Migi jodan no kamae, in pictures 1-3 shikata changes from chudan to gedan, tempting ukekata to attack. In picture 4 ukekata stands in migi jodan and attacks from above, and shikata practices the right timing and angle of the block.

Pictures 5-6: In order to knock down the sword of ukekata with the shinogi, shikata's sword has to move correctly.
Pictures 7-11: After knocking down the opponent's sword, without giving the slightest opening, shikata takes back the sword and strikes.
Picture 11: Receiving instruction on the timing of this strike.

Iai, Muko no kata

1

2

3

4

5

6

7

8

9

10

11

12

Assumption of a hostile act. The enemy strikes from the upper front, Picture 3: after the batto, receive the attack and knock the strike down. Pictures 4-5: Strike the front.

CHAPTER 4

The Famous Schools of Bujutsu

OISHI SHINKAGE-RYU

From the 14th century until the 16th century, many of the ancestors of Bujutsu risked their lives conducting ascetic practices, employing magical techniques and powerful prayers to the Buddha and the Shinto gods. By doing so the figures of the gods would appear or their voices would be heard. Such was the strength of the techniques of these ryuha, they were even able to summon the very gods themselves.

By the 18th century, the warrior had already studied famous techniques that were several hundred years old, and with their own sensitivities had attained the innermost secrets. With this understanding they created new styles, and with those styles developed technique and spirit, rendering the sword techniques more practical.

Even if one does not pray to the gods as Miyamoto Musashi did, through one's willpower and persistency, deadly techniques can accumulate, and new famous styles can be born. One of these styles is the Oishi Shinkage-ryu, also known as the Oishi-ryu.

The founder of this style was Oishi Susumu, who was born to a samurai family. Ever since he was a little child he had learned from his grandfather the sword techniques of Shinkage-ryu. He was once humiliated concerning his kenjutsu skills, after which he resolved to improve his training techniques. He wore a wooden branch as a sword and practiced his stabbing techniques (tsuwaza) to such an extent that he became the preeminent stabbing technique master in Yanagawahan. Uncommon for Japanese, he was around 197cm to 2m tall, so his stabbing technique was performed with specially designed wooden bamboo swords that were 5 or 6 shaku (165cm). With the length of his arm his strikes could reach 2.70-3m.

In 1821 he rose to the position as the head of his family, and around that time it is thought that he refined his techniques into a new independent style. He then went to Edo (today Tokyo) with his lord, and approached many famous ryuha's dojos to challenge them to duels. He fought many times and never lost once.

Because of these duels he gained a reputation as "the dojo destructor." Despite this, he was a very well mannered man who always showed respect for the dojos and demonstrated exceptional etiquette during duels.

As a result, many of the warriors whom he beat, including Chiba Shusaku, Momoi Shunsaku, and Shimada Toranosuke, became good friends with him. His

Yanagawa Castle.

master, daimyo Tachibana, hailed him as a vassal to be proud of, and raised his salary.

Moreover, the reason he started to use a long wooden or bamboo sword was because in the Tachibana clan in which he served, the batto-jutsu (drawing style) of the formerly mentioned Kage-ryu's nodachi (the especially long sword from 165cm-180cm) was passed down. It seems that the influence was very significant.

One day in Nagato (today Yamaguchi prefecture), a warrior named Kurushima Matabeh challenged Oishi to a duel. When the duel started Oishi used the stabbing technique he had perfected, hitting Kurushima's face and accidentally taking Kurushima's eye out. Kurashima survived the duel but was left partially blinded. Three years later, five or six travelling samurai came to Yanagawa. One of them had only one eye. "Did you come seeking revenge?" Oishi asked the man. But the truth was the man and his companions had come in the hope of becoming Oishi's disciples.

Such was the nobility of his techniques and character. The records of the disciples of Oishi indicate that the ancestors of Japan's old prime ministers, Yoshida Shigeru, Asou Taro, and Yoshida Toyo, had all studied the Oishi-ryu. Sakamoto Ryoma had also started studying kenjutsu from Oishi disciple Higuchi Shinkichi. In western Japan and Shikoku, many high-level warriors have entered this ryuha and studied its techniques.

I have also received instructions of these unique sword techniques, from the 5th Soke Shihan, Eiichi Oishi. In the following pictures the secret stabbing technique is shown.

Shinkage-ryu hyoho gojukkajo—an old document that contains all the knowledge and guiding principles of Oishi Shinkage-ryu.

Oishi Susumu's grave.

Soke Oishi (right) and the author.

The greetings before starting practice is a sokourei greeting (touching only with the nails on the ground).

The stances of Oishi Shinkage-ryu kenjutsu

Shinken or Mae chudan.

Mae chudan.

Gedan.

Jodan.

Waki jodan.

Waki chudan.

Kuruma.

Urazuke.

Isshin (omotemen morotezuki)

1

2

3

4

On the left side—the author, on the right side—Oishi soke.
Picture 1: First receiving instructions for Tsuke no kamae.
Picture 2: In the second that author changes to Jodan no kamae, without giving an opening Oishi soke attacks the face with a double-handed stab. (this is a specialty of this style).
Pictures 3-4: The author, seeing the coming attack, tries to knock the opponent's sword down, Oishi soke lifts his sword and with the side of the blade (the shinogi), blocks the strike. The author immediately tries to strike the knees, but also here Oishi soke blocks the strike with the shinogi.

This kind of technique—employing the use of stabbing and blocking—is a very refined and noble way of using a sword. It is taught as the speciality of this style, but also it is a kata that is used to measure or guess the opponent's ability.

Ichimi

1

2

3

4

5

6

7

8

Picture 1: On the left side the author (shitachi), right side Oishi soke (uchidachi), both standing in Jodan no kamae.
Pictures 2-3: Uchidachi strikes straight so shitachi takes one step back and dodges the strike.

Pictures 4-8: Uchidachi immediately goes back to Jodan no kamae and tries to strike again, so while receiving the strike, shitachi bends and strikes the head. End of technique.

Nisho

1

2

3

4

Picture 1: Left side the author (shitachi) stands in Shinken mae chudan no kamae; right side Oishi soke (shitachi) stands in Jodan no kamae.

Picture 2: Uchidachi strikes straight, so shitachi meets the sword with his own sword. Then, as seen in Pictures 3-4, pushes the opponent's sword down and observes the opponent.

In the nisho technique, after pushing down the strike of the opponent, the observation is on his ability. This feature can also be found in other techniques but, being a practice which is backed up with improvement of one's skill and personality (maintaining a high mental state and then pushing the opponent's sword), it makes it a very noble and high level kind of practice. This is the speciality of this style.

Tsuke no kata, a stab between the eyebrows with a long wooden sword – left uchidachi, right shitachi

1

2

3

4

5

6

Picture 1: Usual bokuto (1m), long bokuto (1.5m).
Picture 2: Uchidachi stands in jodan, shitachi in gedan, giving an opening of the upper body, inviting the opponent to attack.
Pictures 3-4: Uchidachi takes the invitation and attacks straight, then shitachi blocks with the shinogi and stabs.
Pictures 5-6: Uchidachi, while stepping back, swings his sword, but he is being threatened by shitachi's sword pointing to his face. The sword does not hit his face and does not harm him, however; this is what makes it such a high-level technique.

Oishi soke, Tsuke no kamae.

KAGE-RYU

The Kage-ryu, which in modern times still effuses an atmosphere of the war period, was created in the year 1610 by Yamamoto Masakatsu. He was taught kenjutsu (fencing) and iaido (sword drawing) by Katayama Houki no kami Hisayau, the sword master of the emperor's chief adviser Toyotomi Hidetsugu. After finishing his studies he collected the nodachi (special long sword) and batto-jutsu techniques, and formed a school that specialized in long swords. This was the start of the Kage-ryu, which is also known as Kage no-ryu.

This ryuha was passed on by the Yanagawa clan that was located in Kyushu. Only the highest ranked warriors were allowed to study this art. The practice of this ryuha was extremely strict, and did not discriminate between children and adults. The practice was conducted with real swords. From the age of six, practitioners would train with an adult-length sword (70cm). At the ages of ten to fourteen the length of the blade was 2 shaku 2 sun (85cm). When turning genfuku (being recognized as an adult at the age of fifteen) the length of the blade was from 3 shaku (90cm) to 4 shaku 3 sun (130cm). The practice aimed to prepare the warriors to be ready for the battlefield at any time.

From the posture of sitting and leaning on the right knee, the enemy comes from the front, there is no time to draw the nodachi. First draw the kodachi (short sword) while standing up, then throw the kodachi on the enemy. Doing so will make him flinch; at precisely that time draw the nodachi and cut him in two.

Shihan Otsuyama uses a nodachi 3 syaku 8 sun (114cm) long, When an enemy quickly approaches, one stands up throwing the short sword at the assailant, then draws the long sword to cut him.

1

2

3

4

5

6

7

8

SHINGYOTO-RYU KENJUTSU

This style was founded by Iba Zesuiken Hideaki, who studied the Yagyu-ryu (Shinkage-ryu) and Honshinto-ryu, and in both schools he received a full license. In 1682 he named his style the Shingyoto-ryu, thereby founding this ryuha. This school still passes on the Enmei-ryu two-sword techniques that were taught to Yagyu Hyogonosuke by Musashi 400 years ago. In the following pages the two-sword techniques and one-sword techniques will be presented.

The purpose of practice: when facing a strong enemy, feelings of fear or desire to avoid the fight might arise in one's heart. This is true for many people. In order to overcome this weakness, continuous training in kenjutsu will help one to develop a strong will. Then, one will understand the true meaning of fighting and will gain fortitude.

Saluting Shihan Masaro Kobayashi.

Shihan Kobayashi (right) and the author.

The dojo of Shingyoto-ryu.

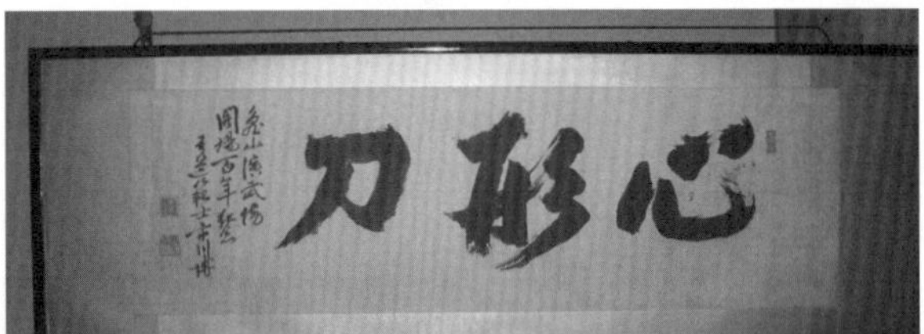

The kanji characters of Shin-gyo-to (read from right to left) in a frame..

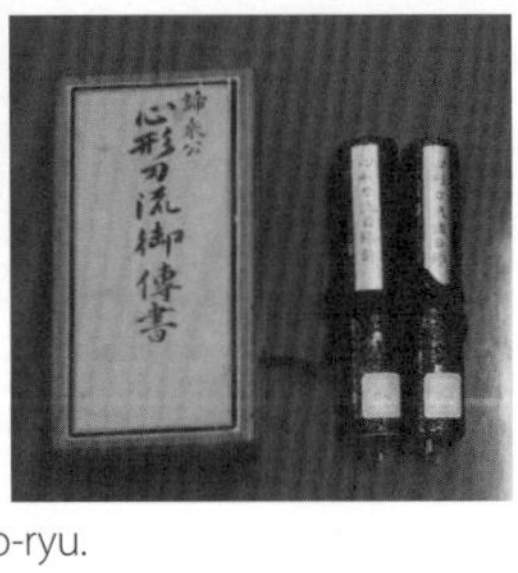

The makimonos of Shingyoto-ryu.

An illustrated secret picture of the ryuha.

Odachi no kumidachi

KASHATO

1

2

3

4

5

6

7

8

9

10

11

The party on the right side is uchidachi. The party on the left is shitachi. Both sides are standing in Jodan no kamae and stepping towards each other. Both sides attack each other in the center simultaneously. Immediately take one step back and stand in Hasso no kamae, again strike simultaneously each other's kesa (diagonally). Without wasting a moment uchidachi attacks above the ankle, shitachi stops him. Again, immediately uchidachi tries to cut the torso from the fight side, but shitachi takes one step left, and strikes uchidachi's right wrist. End of technique.

GOSHATO

1

2

3

4

Uchidachi stands in Jodan no kamae, shitachi in Kuruma no kamae. Shitachi pulls his sword to the right side, and steps forward. Uchidachi strikes straight, shitachi knocks the sword away and cuts uchidachi's neck. End of technique.

Kodachi no kata

NAKAZUNBE-KEN

1

2

3

4

5

6

7

8

9

10

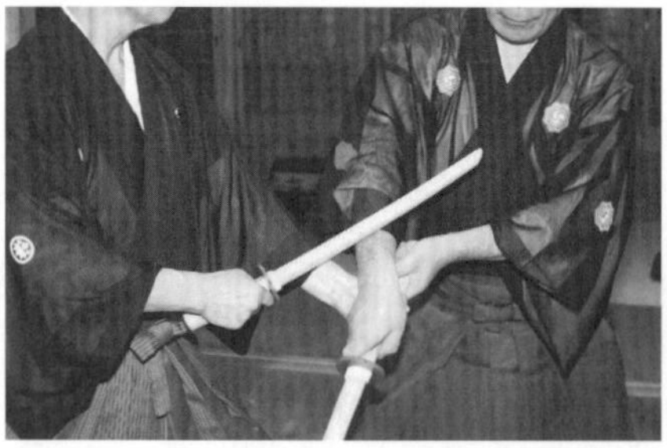
11

12

Uchidachi holds a long sword and stands in Jodan no kamae, shitachi holds a short sword and holds the back of the sword with his left hand and stands in Gedan no kamae. Both sides progress towards each other, uchidachi strikes straight, shitachi blocks the sword and pushes it to the right. Immediately with the left hand holding the center of the tsuka of uchidachi's sword from the bottom, he presses the short sword to the partner's right wrist, then he points the sword to uchidachi's chest. End of technique.

URA NO NAMI

1

2

3

4

5

6

7

8

9

Uchidachi with a long sword stands in Jodan no kamae. Shitachi holds the sword with one hand and stands in jodan. Both sides progress toward each other. Uchidachi strikes straight. In the same second, shitachi strikes with his tsukigashira to the partner's solar plexus. At any point uchidachi is going to strike, so shitachi dodges the strike and hits the wrist. End of technique.

Nito kumitachi

These are the Enmei-ryu two-sword techniques that were passed on to the Yagyu clan by Musashi.

MUKO MANSU (YOKO MANSU)

1

2

3

4

5

6

7

8

9

10

11

12

13

This technique is the same as the shishinoharairi of the Shinkage-ryu.
Uchidachi holds a long sword and moves from chudan to Jodan no kamae, shitachi holds two swords crossed in front and stands in Chudan no kamae.
Both sides progress towards each other. First, uchidachi strikes in order to knock down the crossed swords. Shitachi opens both of his hands, dodges the strike, and immediately using both of the swords he pushes his partner's sword down, then he strikes the front of uchidachi with the long sword. End of technique. Shitachi stretches the long sword to the right, places the short sword in front of his chest, and assumes zanshin.

YOKO MANSU NOKORI (TOAIGIRI) ONE-PERSON PRACTICE

1

2

3

4

5

6

7

8

9

This kata is similar to mukomasu with small changes. This kata is to be practiced by one person.

AIMAKI (SEIGAN YABURI)

1

2

3

4

5

6

7

8

9

10

11

Uchidachi stands in Jodan no kamae, shitachi stands in Chudan no kamae with both swords open. This is a trick designed to tempt the partner to attack. Both sides progress towards each other. Uchidachi strikes straight, and shitachi takes one step back and dodges the strike. Immediately shitachi pushes the partner's sword down with both of his swords, then he strikes the partner's front. End of technique. Shitachi stretches the long sword to the right, places the short sword in front of the chest, and assumes zanshin.

RYUSETSUTO (TAKANOHA)

1

2

3

4

5

6

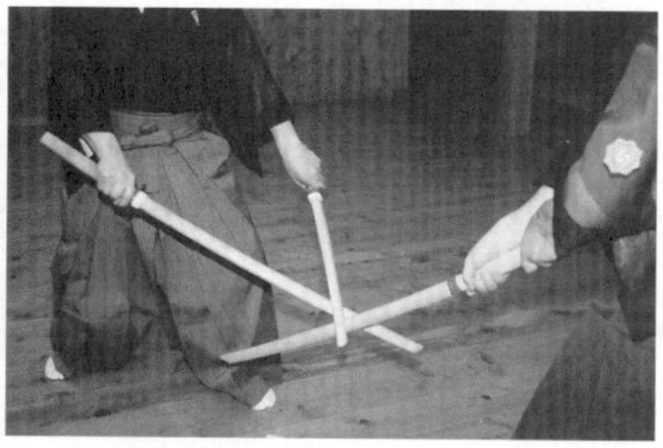

7

8

9

10

11

12

Uchidachi stands in Jodan no kamae, shitachi holds both his swords open and stands in gedan. This is also a trick to tempt the partner to strike. Both sides progress towards each other. Uchidachi strikes straight. Shitachi takes one step back, and spreads his hands like a hawk spreading its wings, by doing so he removes uchidachi's long sword, then immediately he pushes it down with both of his swords. Uchidachi tries again to strike the left wrist, so shitachi hides his left hand behind his back and dodges the strike. With the right hand he strikes the partner's right wrist. End of technique.

SUIGETSUTO (SANSHINTO)

This kata is the same as takanoha with a few changes. It is a practice of hiding the short sword behind the back. This is a one-person practice.

1

2

3

4

5

6

7

MUHYOSHI

Uchidachi stands in Jodan no kamae. Shitachi moves his swords like a hawk flapping its wings, opens his hands, and crosses, inviting the partner. Uchidachi strikes straight, and shitachi uses the short sword to block the strike and at the same time, with the right hand holding the long sword strikes the partner's left wrist. End of technique.

1

2

3

4

5

6

7

8

9

10

SHINTO MUNEN-RYU KENJUTSU

This style was born from an old religion called Haikakyo, whose custom was to light a fire before the gods and to pray devoutly. In 1735, a person called Fukui Hyoemon, who had a licence from a ryuha which was related to the Shinkage-ryu, the Shin shinkage ichien-ryu, went to pray in an old shrine called Izunamyojin. While fasting for several days he prayed to the fire and practiced the ways of Izuna. As a result he became enlightened to the inner secrets of kenjutsu and strategy tactics, and founded the Shinto munen-ryu.

This ryuha became famous in 1788, when one of its disciples had avenged his father's death—from that point the ryuha became esteemed. After that incident, the shihan of the ryuha went all over Japan and taught the techniques, but unlike modern-day kendo, wrist and facial protective gear was not used, so the practice was more akin to real combat, and was known as Sumen-ryu (a ryuha that doesn't use protective gear). In 1800, my ryuha, the Enshin-ryu, took in some parts of those techniques, and merged them with older techniques. These newly developed techniques are passed on until this day.

Towards the end of the Warring Period, when Japan was ravaged by battles between the government and rebel armies, swordsmen who trained in this ryuha all took part in the wars. It is said that these swordsmen went to the front line, and without considering if the enemy was near or far, drew their swords while entering a mental state of mushin, and ran, swinging their blades. Only when they noticed that their swords had hit some metal which might have been part of the enemy's weapon did they check how many people they had killed or whether or not they had been wounded.

This style, this powerful kenjutsu way of thinking, holds that the sword obeys the movement of the hand, the hand obeys the command of the mind, the mind obeys kenjutsu and the ryuha's law, and the ryuha's law obeys the will of the gods. When one makes progress, the sword, the hand, and the mind are forgotten, one enters a mental state of freedom from all thought or distraction, and with the guidance of the gods one enters the world of oneness with nature.

Soke Takeshi Ogawa.

Goka gogyo no kata

1

2

3

4

5

6

7

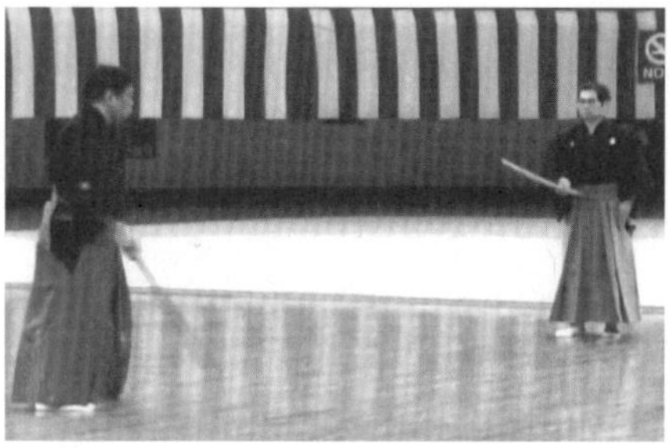
8

9

10

11

12

13

14

15

16

17

The gokagogyo has five versions in its basic form. Here the most basic one is presented.
Pictures 1-7: Uchidachi and shitachi make a greeting standing. According to the law of the ryuha the bokuto is placed on the ground, and mokushi is preformed (watching your opponent silently). Next, without taking their eyes off their partners, both parties pick up the bokuto. Uchidachi on the left stands in Hasso no kamae and watches carefully while shitachi stands in Chudan no kamae. Next, uchidachi changes the stance to Chudan no kamae, shitachi releases his right hand from the bokuto and takes five steps back.
Pictures 7-18: Uchidachi strikes straight from hasso no kame, shitachi also strikes so it becomes a simultaneous strike, and immediately they strike again. Then, uchidachi tries to push shitachi's sword, so shitachi pushes back. Shitachi puts his sword on the sword of uchidachi and steps forward, and stabs with suigetsu. End of technique.

JIKI SHINKAGE-RYU KENJUTSU

The characteristic of this style is that strength and body movement in the techniques are brought to a maximum. The basics of the sword techniques are to start from a daijodan and hit the partner from above with all one's power. This is why there were many cases of bruises and fractures when practicing these techniques, and sometimes people even became permanently injured. It was extremely important to protect the head and face, and also the hands and wrists.

After lengthy research of protective equipment, at the beginning of the 18th century, the original form of the equipment that is now used in kendo was put to practical use. Thereafter the nakanishiha of the Itto-ryu adopted and improved the wrist and torso protective equipment. Since the practice became safer, many new disciples entered the school and it became very successful. However, these days, without using protective gear, the Jiki shinkage-ryu successors are passing on the dignified, majestic, original techniques in their true form.

Greeting between the author (in black) and Kazuya Namiki Shihan.

Techniques:
This ryuha is based on techniques that have their roots in old Shinto, before Buddhism arrived in Japan. The old Shinto faith believes that everything starts and ends with breathing. With the strength of prayer and the strength of faith in the gods, one acts. The practice uniforms for this school are white like the Shinto priests' daily clothes, and its practitioners, with devotion to old Shinto in their hearts, would aspire to be one with the gods, or to reach a state in which a god has entered their bodies and made their hearts as solid and strong as an iron wall.

Hojo no kata Itto ryodan

1

2

3

4

5

6

7

8

9

10

11

12

13

14

15

16

17

18

19

20

In this kata, as with many from this school, start by making your partner fear you and sharpening your spirit. Then, without hesitating, strike with all your strength and devotion. From this point emerges the dignified virtue that was born from Shinto, and the noble, uncompromising refinement is manifested in oneself.

Kodachi Fusei

1

2

3

4

5

6

7

8

9

10

11

12

13

14

15

The kodachi is a short sword, and challenging to a duel against long swords or other weapons is a practice of courage. One's heart should remain strong and one should never underestimate the importence of technique.

Uchidachi uses a daito (long sword) and shitachi uses a kodachi (short sword). Shitachi throws all his fear away, and forgetting the fear of death holds his sword and stands. Then, with the power of a kamikaze (godly wind), he runs in a straight line forward and hits uchidachi with a triumphant strike.

Kodachi Toppi ohi

1

2

3

4

5

6

7

8

9

10

11

12

13

14

15

In this technique uchidachi uses a dato and shitachi uses a kodachi. Uchidachi attacks, and shitachi receives the attack and counter-strikes. Uchidachi backs off and stands in Jodan. Shitachi bows on his left leg, touches the floor with his left hand, and stretches his right leg forward, making the enemy think that he is tired and inviting him to strike. Then uchidachi is fooled into thinking that shitachi has lost his self control, and, seeing this situation he attacks. Shitachi blocks the attack and counter-strikes. Uchidachi backs up and stands in jodan, the technique is repeated one more time, crossing the swords, and both of the parties stand in chudan. End of technique.

THE LINEAGE OF ITTO-RYU

The martial arts were created to teach followers how to survive on the battlefield, by having life or death struggles, studying unbeatable secret techniques, and reaching a level of mastery that if one fights he will always win. This was the first target of the martial arts. In order to check one's skills, duels and fights with other ryuhas were often held, and by winning those fights, one could gain recognition from society. This was one means of becoming successful. This way of thinking was observed across all schools of the martial arts, and indeed across much of society at the time, from the military to the merchant class. Understanding the importance of the tradition of Japanese culture, the hardest task was to choose a successor of a kenjutsu ryuha.

Many of the martial arts were born around the 16th century, during the later years of the Warring Period. In those times the principle of competition was at the core of the martial arts. Concepts like yushorepai (the superior wins, the inferior loses), or jakunikukyoshoku (the weak are the prey and the strong are the predators) were common, and those who could win in a duel had a chance to survive and prosper. On the other hand, if one lost he would die and lose everything—if it was a ryuha it would disappear, if it was a merchant family it would go bankrupt; that was the harsh reality of those days.

Thus, just as Miyamoto Musashi was the adopted child of Miyamoto Munisai, each ryuha would only hand down its secrets to very strong and outstanding individuals when considering its own development and permanence. Consider the craft of pottery—if a potter's work is inferior and contains the slightest defect he would destroy it, and would only preserve his best craftsmanship for use in his trade.

The same is true in the martial arts world—only the very best disciples would be able to continue the traditions and hand down the techniques of the school. If, for example, a devotee of the martial arts displays vanity and progresses slowly in his studies, or seeks out enemies and shows belligerent behaviour, this is a sign that his upbringing was poor. In extreme cases, to ensure such a practitioner wouldn't leave behind any bad traditions, the teacher would give him a shinken (real sword) and, under the guise of teaching him "secret techniques," would kill him. Moreover, anyone who looked at the secret techniques, scrolls, or old books without permission would be cut down in that very instant.

The ryuha introduced here, the Itto-ryu, has a long history of very strict, harsh

Mikogami Tenzen Tadaaki.

Ito Ittosai Kagehisa.

ways of choosing its successors. The founder of this ryuha, Ito Itosai Kagehisa, chose the successor of his ryuha by forcing his two best disciples, Mikogami Tenzen and Ono Zenki, into a duel in which only the winner would succeed the ryuha. His disciples obeyed their teacher's orders; Tenzen won the duel and Zenki lost his life.

It is unknown what happened to Ito Ittosai Kagehisa after passing down the ryuha to Mikogami Tenzen, and the time and place of his death is also a mystery. Perhaps he died in the middle of some fields and mountains with no funeral, just exposed to the weather, slowly returning to mother earth. It is thought that he died in a very ancient, ideal Japanese way.

In order to manage the kenjutsu ryuha without any compromise, Mikogami Tenzen had killed other fellow disciples, and later adopted the family name of Ono Zenki, changing his name to Ono Jiroemon Tadaki. Later, in 1593, he became, on the recommendation of either Ittosai or Yagyu Munenori, a kenjutsu instructor of the Tokugawa shogun.

The special technical feature of this ryuha is fighting against a large number of warriors. It doesn't matter how many enemies one is faced with, the secret techniques teach how to cut them down one after the other. The basic technique is actually the inner secret named "kiri otoshi," a technique in which both sides strike each other down; this technique is connected to another stabbing technique.

In this kenpo technique, two effects result from executing one movement—the opponent is cut while, at the same time, a stabbing technique naturally happens. This movement is truly very simple, so even an amateur can imitate it. Without the shihan level training, however, "namabyoho wa kega no moto" can occur; a phrase that means if beginners can execute a simple movement, they should not think their skill is too high, because if they try something more complicated they may injure themselves, so caution is necessary. Moreover, the practice in Itto-ryu is carried out with shinken (real swords) as a principle but, in order to avoid injury, a habiki (a sword blunted on the whetstone) is used.

The grandson of Ono Jiroemon Tadaaki continued as the instructor of the Tokogawa shogunate but, after the Meiji Restoration the Ono clan ceased to be swordsmen.

In the 18th century Nakanishi Chuta, who received a full license from the Ono clan, started promoting the Nakanishiha Itto-ryu. This ryuha is recognized as having designed the protective wear for modern kendo. His dojo gained great prosperity, and it is said he had more than 8,000 disciples.

A warrior called Asari Matashichiro Yoshinobu, who studied Nakanishiha Itto-ryu, promoted the school as Asariha Itto-ryu, and from this ryuha Hokushin Itto-ryu and Ittoshoden muto-ryu were born. These two ryuha had a big influence on today's modern Budo. The promoters of Asariha Itto-ryu had studied from the adopted child of Asari Yoshinobu, Asari Matashichiro Yoshiaki. Their names are still well known: Chiba Shusaku and Yamaoka Tesshu. Chiba Shusaku was just a simple *ronin*, until he merged the Itto-ryu with a ryuha that was founded by his father called Hokushin Muso-ryu, and called this new ryuha Hokushin Itto-ryu. By promoting this new ryuha he gained recognition as a top class warrior.

The main lesson that Chiba taught for his new ryuha was that the rhythm of practice was inspired by the movement of the tail of a wagtail (sekirei). Even in simple practice when crossing swords, the high tension can cause the arm to become stiff and one might not use the sword the way one would like to. Chiba maintained that while using the sword, imitating the movement of the tail of a wagtail helps to ease the tension and one can use the sword freely. This technique is called Sekirei no ken (the wagtail's sword).

Moreover, when the modern era began in Japan, two of the students of the Hokushin Itto-ryu who received a full license, Naito Takaharu and Monna Tadashi, made a great contribution to the development of modern kendo, and their names are still known today. The Hokushin Itto-ryu is the source of modern day kendo. It is said that the kendo practiced these days in Japan is succeeding the spirit of Bushido, but there are arguments against this theory.

In the aftermath of World War II, the general headquarters of the occupation forces gave an authorization to make sports like shinai (kendo sword) duel, and that was the time when the sport version of Budo came into the world. It is fair to say that modern kendo is not connected to the traditional ryuhas Hokushin Itto-ryu and Onoha Itto-ryu, and has no common ground with Bushido.

ONOHA ITTO-RYU

Seigan.

The "Kiri otoshi" technique is so strong that it can cut down in one strike the wrist, arm, or the back of the hand. It can even cut a sword. When the opponent stands in Jodan no kamae immediately strike him down.

Gedan seigan.

Oni gote (big splints).

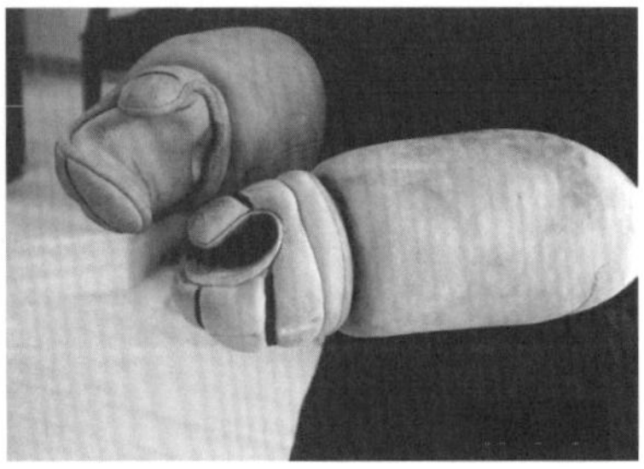

Wearing oni gote splints on the arms.

Migi jodan kamae.

Throat stabbing technique.
From the chest to the lower stomach, without using the hands but the body, after cutting a stabbing technique is performed.

Onken no kamae.

In no kamae.

Kongo no kamae.

Yo no kamae.

In no kamae.

Finishing the practice and saluting together.

Practicing in the dojo.

Kiri otoshi no kata

1

2

3

4

5

6

7

8

9

Itto-ryu's "kiri otoshi" technique was the first technique taught to disciples who were allowed to enter the school, and after learning all the techniques of the ryuha, it was taught again as an inner secret technique.

The person in white is uchidachi, and in black is shitachi.

Picture 1: Both sides stand in Aiseigan no kamae.

Picture 2: Uchidachi changes his stance to hasso, in order to attack.

Pictures 3-5: Uchidachi strikes; in response shitachi also strikes and with the side of the blade ("shinogi"), hits uchidachi's blade and aims the sword to the throat, so at any second he can stab the opponent down.

Pictures 6-7: In order to attack again uchidachi takes a step back with his right leg, and stands in jodan, then shitachi, without losing a second, strikes with a "kiriotoshi." At that point it doesn't matter if the opponent has fencing gloves or not; shitachi has to cut down the enemy's wrist in one cut.

Picture 8: Shitachi cuts down from the solar plexus into the lower stomach, until he stands in Gedan seigan no kamae. The secret of this technique is that the power of the strike does not come from the strength of the hands but from the movement of the legs.

Picture 9: Both parties return to Seigan no kamae. End of technique.

At the end of the practice, the fencing gloves are taken off and both parties bow to each other.

HOKUSHIN ITTO-RYU

Chiba Shusaku, the school founder.

Master Jujiro Konishi the predecessor Soke.

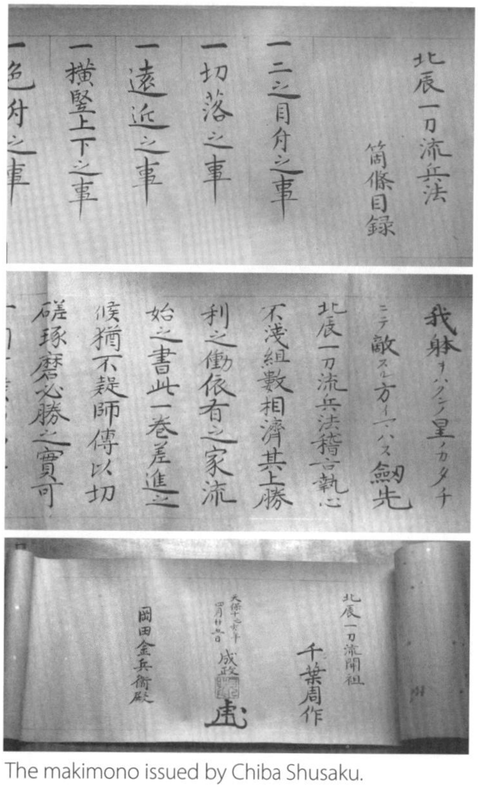

The makimono issued by Chiba Shusaku.

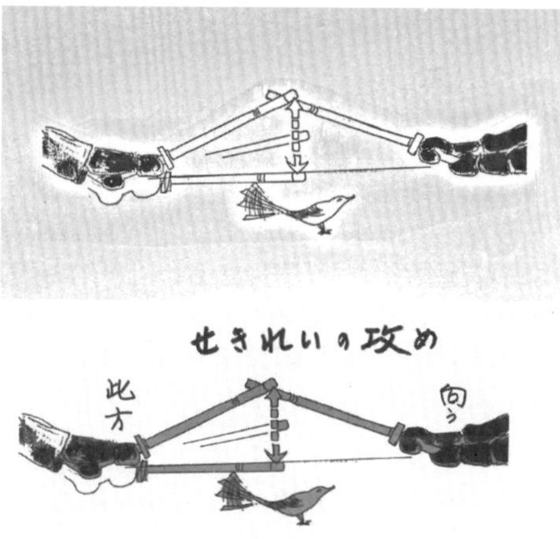

Illustrated instructions of Sekirei kenpo (wagtail movements of the sword) written and drawn by the late Soke Konishi.

Practicing in the dojo.

ITTO SHODEN MUTO-RYU

Next, Itto shoden muto-ryu will be introduced. This style was founded by Yamaoka Tesshu. He studied Nakanishiha Itto-ryu and Asariha Itto-ryu, among others. He also deeply practiced Zen. From his early years to his prime, it was a very turbulent period in Japan's history. After 267 years of national isolation the Tokugawa regime's political power was beginning to break, the political leaders were losing their mandates, and the international wind that was blowing did not fit with the regime's way of thinking. Yamaoka at that time was a low-class warrior for the Tokugawa shogunate, but he had a vision of returning to the emperor and the royal family and building a new Japan.

In 1868, towards the end of the era when authority was held by warriors wielding swords, a war started between the emperor's new government forces and the shogunate army. The Tokugawa clan, however, lost the battle in just one day and fled back to Edo. In the midst of these times Yamaoka Tesshu was promoted to become the representative of the shogunate and to negotiate with the new government. He went to the headquarters of the new government carrying his short sword, without carrying his long sword. He met with the commanding officer Saigo Takamori, and reached an agreement which stated that by handing over Edo Castle he would save the city from being burned to the ground. Yamaoka started working in national affairs, and worked as a chamberlain for the Meiji Emperor. He was awarded the equivalent rank of a viscount in the old nobility system.

Yamaoka Tesshu studied the Asariha Itto-ryu and received a full license. With the onset of the Meiji era, however, he went to the Ono clan, and studied the original Itto-ryu, known as Onoha Itto-ryu, and alternated between the kenjutsu kata of both styles.

While diligently practicing the martial arts, one should aspire to attain perfection of one's technique. More important than this, however, is mental practice. When fear enters the heart, it is because hope and courage have been lost. In Budo this is looked upon as a disease. Yamaoka studied a technique to overcome this disease. In ancient Japanese Shinto the most basic ceremony is to wash one's body with pure water a number of times. This is called "kansui no ho" (the technique of watering). After purifying the body, a special method of breathing called "susokukan," the purifying of the inner body, is used. Furthermore, in order to purify the mind and soul, a practice of Zen is performed. This practice is called

Yamaoka Tesshu, the school founder.

"semui," reaching a state of mind where there is no fear; reaching the state of "mushin" (no mind).

One of the endearing aspects of Japanese martial arts is that with the training of the techniques the student also learns about religious philosophies like Buddhism, among others. By doing that the teacher aims to cultivate his students to a high level, and when they attain the level of master, the technical and spiritual teachings are transmitted together. This way of thinking is akin to that of a head priest of a certain religion, who passes on that faith with the hope of fostering a world free from fighting. As a master of his art, with a high intellect and a respected personality, Yamaoka Tesshu succeeded in capturing the concept of "wa no geijutsu" (the Japanese art), and founded Itto Shoden muto-ryu, and passed it to future generations.

THE HISTORY OF YAGYU SHINGAN-RYU

Very little is known of the origins of this style, but it is said to be founded by Yagyu Gorobee in the 16th century. In the 17th century, however, Takenaga Hayato, who was a student of Yagyu Tajima No kami Munenori, received a full license, and was allowed to bear the ryuha's name. From that point on the ryuha was blessed with many illustrious individuals who have handed down its martial and spiritual techniques until this day. Furthermore, at the end of the Edo era, one of its shihans, Hoshi Teikichi, became famous for avenging his father's death, a deed that carried great honor in those days. His act not only bestowed upon Hoshi Teikichi great honor but also made this ryuha famous.

Kotenuki

1

2

3

4

5

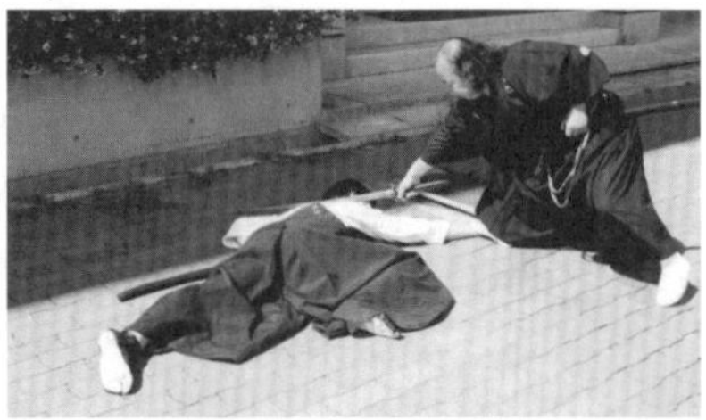

6

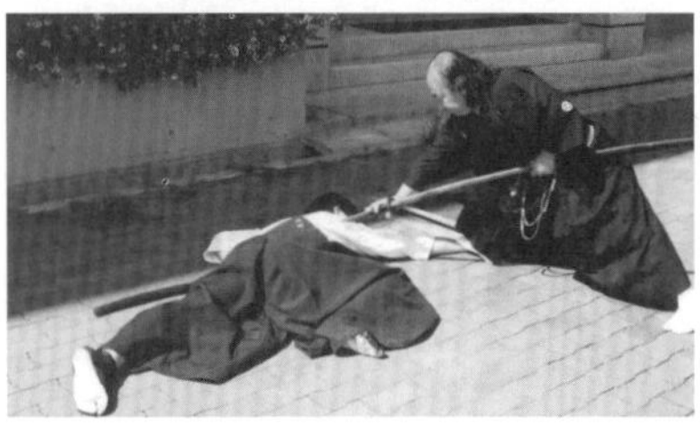

7

8

Party A moves his body to a half-body position, and shows his right shoulder in order to tempt party B to attack and move into his kamae. When party A steps towards party B, party B pulls back in order to draw the sword, and immediately party A steps in with his left leg and using his tsuba (the sword handle) pushes party B's right wrist so he cannot draw his sword. Then, holding party B's right wrist using the tsuka (hilt), party A pushes party B's right arm, pulling the wrist so party B falls.
Using the tsuka party A pushes party B's shoulder so he is unable to move. Then, party A draws his sword by pulling and cuts to the neck.

The Yagyu-ryu technique's arsenal has a wide variety: armor fighting, hook (a kind of spear), kenjutsu, yari (spear), naginata, scythe, kusarigama (sickle and chain), and many more. The bedrock of the army—the low-class soldiers who fought on the battlefield—had to study this style. From the many techniques of this ryuha, a few techniques of kenjutsu and nito kodachi (two short swords) will be introduced in this book—with special thanks to Kenji Shimazu Shihan.

Kotenuki (detailed explanation of the first four pictures)

1

2

3

4

Party A moves his body to a half-body (hanmi) position, and shows his right shoulder in order to tempt party B to attack and move into his kamae. When party A steps forward party B will be showing his shoulder, party B pulls back in order to draw the sword, immediately party A steps in with his left leg and pushes with his tsuba (the sword handle) and pushed party B's right wrist so he cannot draw his sword. Until this picture (no.4).
This technique's feature is the point when party A presents his shoulder making Party B want to attack, then when party B wants to draw, using a technique on the wrist, arm and shoulder party A can gain control of him.

Kagefusa-no-tachi (front kata) Sageo no sabaki

1

2

3

4

5

6

7

8

9

10

Both parties draw the swords from kamae, then party A holds the sword with the right hand and pulls the saya from the obi (belt) with the left hand. When party B attacks, party A, with his left hand holding the saya, using the string wraps party B's sword and pulls it; with the right hand he cuts from the left and then again cuts back to the right side and cuts party B's right part of the neck.

Kagefusei-no-tachi (back kata)

1

2

3

4

5

6

7

8

Party A stands in hanmi, holding the saya to his back so it will be hidden. When party B attacks from the front, Party B blocks the hit with the sword and at the same time with his left hand whips the face of party B with the string of the saya (sageo). With the sword and the saya he drops party B's sword to the ground. Then immediately with the right hand he cuts and then again takes the sword back and cuts the neck.

Nito kodachi (Hatten no kata)

1

2

3

4

5

6

Party A holds two short swords and stands in Hatten no kamae. Party B attacks from the front. Party A, while blocking the sword with his right hand, takes a step forward with the left leg and cuts with the left hand to party B's wrist.

Nito kodachi (Tenchi in'yo no kata)

1

2

3

4

Party A stands in Tenchi in'yo no kamae. Party B attacks from the front, and while blocking the sword with the left hand, steps forward with the right leg and with the right hand sword cuts the wrist, and pushes.

Nito kodachi (Suihei no kata)

1

2

3

4

5

6

7

Party A stands in Suihei no kamae placing his left hand on eye level. Party B starts from Kuruma no kamae. Then, party A takes his left hand down and opens his upper body for a hit from party B. Party B attacks form above. Party A blocks the hit from the bottom. Party B tries to enter with an attack with the lower part of the sword (tsuka), but party A uses the right hand to block this attack also, and kick him in the torso. After party B falls party A cuts him.

Nito kodachi (Gyaku dachi)

1

2

3

4

5

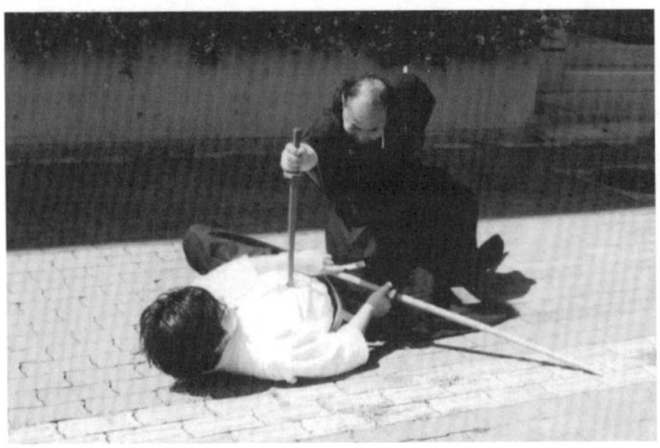

6

7

Party A holds his swords with both hands and hides them behind his back. Party B, from Kuruma no kamae, moves to jodan in order to strike from above. Party A crosses the swords and blocks the hit. To prevent party B from changing his stance Party A uses the tsubamoto (sword base) to fix the sword and kicks the torso. Party B falls, and party A stabs with the right hand.

TENNEN RISHIN-RYU

In the Kansei period (around 1780-90), a country samurai named Kondou Kuranosuke Nagahiro studied the techniques of Shinto-ryu and received a full licence. He had studied a little from other ryuha, and founded a first-class ryuha, which he called the Tennen rishin-ryu. The warriors who studied this ryuha were known as "doushi." They were farmer warriors, or "ronin"—people that originally were warriors but had become masterless. Such warriors trained hard in kenjutsu, holding out a strong hope that one day they would be valued as legitimate warriors in samurai society. In the year 1853 the American navy forced Japan to open its gates, which marked the beginning of the end of the samurai period, and the start of Japan's modernization. From that time, revolutionist warriors from all across Japan gathered in Kyoto in order to overthrow the Tokugawa regime. They started making threatening radical actions, and stability throughout the country worsened.

The Tennen rishin-ryu is especially famous because many of its students were part of a garrison called "Shinsengumi," which the Tokugawa government had organized by recruiting superior ronin in order to suppress the violent revolutionists and to keep the peace in the streets of Kyoto. The second chief of this bureau was the third soke of Tennen rishin-ryu, Kondo Isami. The vice chiefs were Hijikata Toshizo and Okita Shoji, and all of the management had licenses from this ryuha.

The Shinsengumi recruited ambitious warriors and imposed very strict rules on its members. By doing so they managed to guard the city of Kyoto. In addition, if a soldier committed a serious violation of the rules he would be ordered to perform seppuku; if he ran away he would be pursued, brought back, and ordered again to carry out seppuku. If he refused he would be cut down. The Shinsengumi would also target revolutionaries and their own former members for surprise attacks, ambushing them, sometimes even while they slept.

An infamous incident took place in a hotel called the Ikedaya in 1865. The Shinsengumi raided twenty revolutionary warriors who were hiding in the hotel, killing most of them, or wounding them so severely that there was no chance they could be active again. It is said that Shinsengumi delayed the modernization of Japan for ten years. This fearful government-approved hit squad was extremely active, and was highly esteemed; they became formal retainers of the Tokugawa government, and were regarded as real warriors.

The prestige of becoming a formal warrior, however, didn't last long. In 1868 in Toba and Fushimi at the gates of Kyoto, the revolutionary army and the Tokugawa government forces engaged in battle, which ended in victory for the revolutionists in less than two days. The defeated shogun, Tokugawa Yoshinobu, fled back to Edo. The Shinsengumi who took part in this battle were also destroyed; their activity was terminated after only six years.

Kondo Isami fled back to Edo with Hijikata Toshizo and the other warriors who survived. There he changed his name to Ookudo Yamato. He became the general of an army called Koyo chinbutai, and went to fight in Katsunuma, which is in Kai (Yamanashi prefecture), against the revolutionary army. He fought in many battles, and in Shimousa (Chiba prefecture) on Nagareyama he was captured. Although Kondo Isami had hoped for a glorious warrior's death by committing seppuku, he was denied this honor, and instead was beheaded as a farmer in Itabashi in Tokyo. His head was put on display on a pole in Kawara in Kyoto.

The vice chief Hijikata Toshizo took advantage of the confusion of the battlefield and escaped to Hakodate, which is on the northern sea road. In 1869 he fought in the Goryokaku war, and died a warrior's death.

The Shinsengumi and Tennen rishin-ryu, and Kondo, Hijikata, and Okita Soshi, are still very famous names in Japan's history. Sadly this famous ryuha has now disappeared, and its techniques are lost. It is possible, however, to research using old scrolls and books, and revive the old techniques, and there is extensive research into this ryuha being carried out these days.

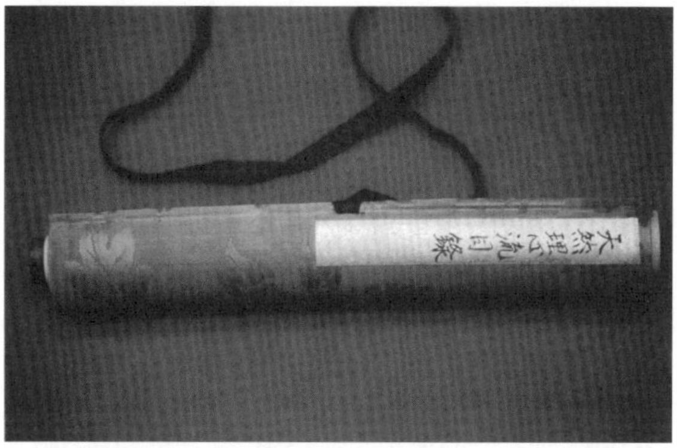

The secret makimono of Tennen rishin-ryu.

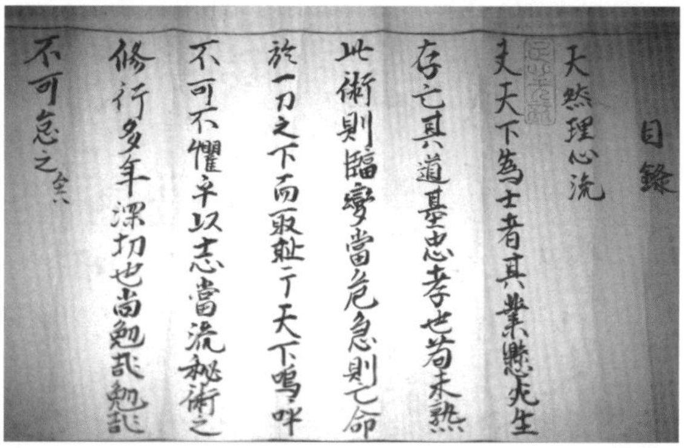
目録
天然理心流
夫天下為士者其業懸先生
存亡其道基忠孝也苟未熟
此術則臨變當危急則亡命
於一刀之下而取耻于天下嗚呼
不可不懼乎以志當流秘術之
修行多年深切也尚勉哉勉哉
不可怠之矣

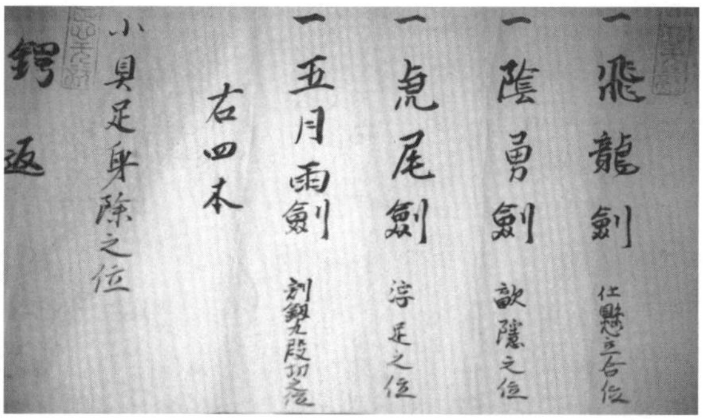
一 飛龍剣
一 陰勇剣
一 虎尾剣 浮足之位
一 五月雨剣
右四本
小具足身除之位
鍔返

寛永十三 中沢兵部 家次
中沢兵部 家正
延宝七 中沢兵部
正徳四 中沢兵部 家吉
八代惣之助 光房
八代惣之助

MUGAI-RYU

In the initial essence of Bujutsu, if one contests in a duel and wins he will live long and might attain self satisfaction, and will also fill a great void in himself. But if he loses he will fall into great despair, and nothing will be left. The warrior had to live in the constant awareness that it is one who will kill first or will be killed, so a state of spiritual peace was the most difficult thing to achieve.

Seeking release from this constant danger and feelings of emptiness, the warriors searched various religions—ancient Shinto, mountain religions, esoteric Buddhism, and common Buddhism. By practicing these religions one would would enter the inner world of calmness and understand the true essence of the fight.

In order to discover the inner secrets, a warrior would learn high-level techniques which could allow him to win no matter who he fights. A warrior would also study deep philosophy. Thus, Bujutsu became also a path that develops a high intellect. This is what is known as "bun bu ichi tai" (technique and study at the same time)—the two paths of technique and intellect have become one. One person who managed to grasp this inner secret as a way of life was the founder of Mugai-ryu, Tsuji Gettan Shigemochi.

He was born in 1649 in Masugi mura, which was known as a ninja village of the Koga county; a house of "doshi" farmer warriors. Aspiring to a path of Bujutsu, he studied with Yamaguchi Bokushinsai learning the Yamagichi-ryu, and received a full license. In addition, he studied with Taga Jikyoken Morimasa, learning the iai technique of Jikyo-ryu, and in 1675 he received a full license. (What is known today as Mugai-ryu iai is actually Jikyo-ryu iai.)

After he received ancient Japanese Bujutsu licenses, he started to search for a path in mental techniques in order to attain total calmness. At the beginning he practiced the faith of the yamabushi (mountain warriors) and the ninjas, the sangaku shukyo (the mountain religion), but after he practiced Zen, he finally attained the truth which in Buddhism is known as "Ge." He entered the mental state of nothingness and received the name Mugai (no outer), so he named his school Mugai-ryu.

The concept of the mental state of nothingness refers to a state in which one's mind is strong, pure, and can't be unbalanced easily. In Zen this is called "semui"—knowing that one's heart has no fear in it. This is an inner secret in Bujutsu which is known as "Godo." The Buddhist truth known as Godo starts with a doctrine that states that human's intellect and power of understanding is influenced by the six senses. This is known as nine-consciousness doctrine, and this is a basic philosophy, but for followers of monotheistic religions, this radical religious philosophy is a little hard to grasp.

In the 20th century the Austrian psychologist Sigmund Freud and his disciple Yung expounded extremely deep psychological theories, but it seems that their theories were limited because they were born from monotheistic religions. Buddhism, being polytheistic, had discovered this deep psychological understanding 3,000 years ago, and had spread it in Japan; therefore I will explain it simply. The doctrine starts with the theory of the six senses, which is called in Japanese "rokkon."

Ganshiki (the eye consciousness); the consciousness of all things that are seen by the eye.

Jishiki (the ear consciousness); the consciousness of all things heard by the ear.

Bishiki (the nose consciousness); the consciousness of all things smelled by the nose.

Zesshiki (the tongue consciousness); the consciousness of food and all things that are tasted by the tongue.

Shinshiki (the body consciousness); the consciousness of things that the body touches.

Ishiki (also called ikon) is the information from all the other consciousnesses, being analyzed in a split second.

Using only these six bases in order to make a judgement of value, in the eyes of the ordinary person this is wisdom, However, outstanding people have another consciousness beyond these six. They have a 7th consciousness, which is called manashiki, which is a deep psychological consciousness, considering things on the societal and public level, and concerning moral judgements.

However, the judgements emanating from the place of the 7th consciousness are not perfect and enlightened; there is still an 8th consciousness known as "ganzoshiki" (arayashiki), which is the entrance to the world of enlightenment. This means not suffering by trying to judge if things are good or bad, but just seeing things as they truly are, and being able to have a clear judgement; in this way the land of enlightenment can be entered. Through Zen practice one can overcome the suffering of one's own weaknesses and ignorance, and exist in a place where the mind is still. Tsuji Gettan may have entered this place. The Zen and the Shingonmikyo sect state that once a person enters the ganzoshiki and the arayashiki, he reaches total enlightenment.

However, if a person achieves enlightenment once but has a weak side in his heart, he may not practice correctly, and might be stained by the world of suffering and worries. The Tendaishu sect has a training method of entering the depth of the 9th consciousness in order to overcome this mental illness, and to exist in the immortal, enlightened mind.

This practice is called "senjou no niho," and it said that if one should continue this practice, the mind will always be strong, right, and pure, but if one should stop the practice out of inertia his mind will be polluted by the common world. Therefore, because the practice had crossed through whole lifetimes, Bushido's intellect had arrived at a level that others could not follow.

The founder of Mugai-ryu, Tsuji Gettan, served as an officer (thereby becoming an official warrior) in the Yamanouchi clan in Tosa (today Kochi precture). As a martial artist and a follower of Zen he didn't have any children, so he adopted one of his students to inherit his legacy. In recent years there have been problems and some lack of clarity as to who should be the current soke, but Mr. Misakazu Konishi strives to succeed this ryuha.

Tsuji Gettan with a wooden sword in his hand.

Tsuji Gettan in Zen practice.

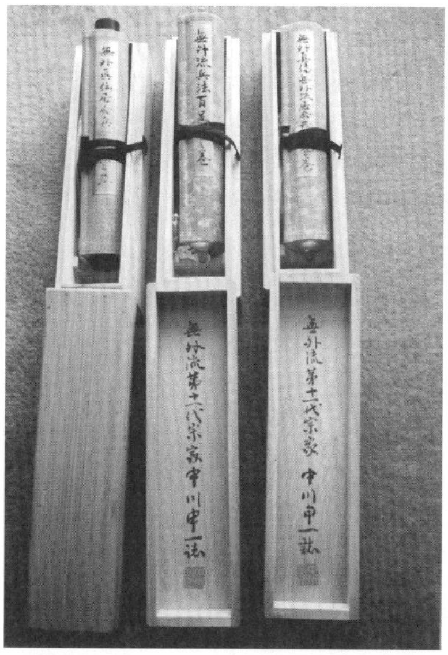

The three makimonos of Mugai-ryu, owned by Soke Konishi.
Owning three makimonos of "Men no maki," "Hyakusoku no maki," and "Kaiden no maki" together is needed to be a master of this school.

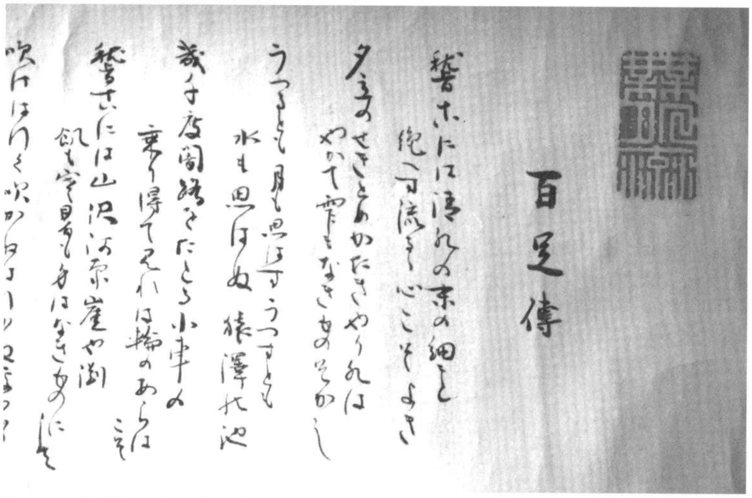

The scroll of "Hyakusoku den."

MANIWA NEN-RYU

This style was founded in the 14th century by a warrior called Somashiro Yoshimoto. It is the oldest distinguished traditional ryuha. When Somashiro was five years old his father was murdered, and his own life also was in danger so he fled from his homeland. As the years passed his thoughts of revenge grew stronger. First he went to Kamakura (today Kangawa-ken, Kamakura City) and studied with a great Buddhist priest, learning the two magic techniques known as "kako" (past), and "genzai" (present).

It is recorded that when he was eighteen years old, he met a mountain warrior who taught him the art of myojutsu in Kuramayama, Kyoto. In 1368 he returned to his homeland and avenged his father's death. The myojutsu and magic techniques that Somashiro had learned in Kamakura and in Kuramayama indicate that the primitive form of Japanese Bujutsu was mainly spells. One prays hard to the gods, and summons them like a shaman. When the power of belief is converted to concrete power it is called magic, or spells of witchcraft.

I hold many of the Shinto secret scrolls concerning magic and sorcery. In order to improve combat instincts, one prays intensely to the various Shinto gods and the Buddhist guardian gods, until he reaches a state of possession, which he maintains until he kills his enemy. The old tradition says that when these techniques are taught, if someone is watching the practice without permission, he must be immediately killed.

After Somashiro had enacted his revenge, he devoted his life to Buddhism, and went on pilgrimages around Japan, and by doing so he achieved enlightenment. In 1408 he changed his name to Nenami Jion and founded his own temple, and since that day the style was called Nen-ryu.

Jion raised fourteen excellent students, but of these the best was Higuchitaro Kaneshige. Higuchitaro was the second successor of the ryuha, and it was passed down through his descendants. But the 4th successor, Higuchi Shinzaemonnojo Takashige had settled down in Joshu (today Gunma-ken), which is in the Maniwa district, so he changed the name of the ryuha to Maniwa nen-ryu, and since then the ryuha has been passed down in the Higuchi clan for over six hundred years.

Nen-ryu was founded because the founder Jion wanted to avenge his father's death. Three hundred years later in the 17th century, a samurai who received full license from this ryuha twice achieved in his life what is known as the flower of Bushido, "adauchi"—the act of revenge. This person was a ronin named Nakayama

Yasube'e. One day, his grandfather, who was a warrior by nature, became embroiled in a fight, and at some point a situation arose in which he had to single-handedly fight against several men. He sent a letter to Yasube'e requesting help.

Yasube'e, however, was a big drinker, and on the day of the duel he got drunk, fell asleep, and didn't make it to the fight. When he finally awoke he dashed to the location of the fight only to find out that his grandfather had been struck down. While his assailants were preparing to leave, he challenged them to another fight. In this fight he used all the Nen-ryu secret sword techniques and avenged his grandfather's death. By avenging his grandfather's death in such a dramatic way, he was highly praised.

The daimyo of Banshu (today Hyogo prefecture), Kashin Horibe Yahei, who was part of the Asano clan, had seen the incident had decided that he wanted Yasube'e as his son-in-law and married him to his daughter. Yasube'e changed his name to Horibe Yasube'e and became an official warrior. Just a few years later on March 14th in 1702, an incident occurred that changed his life dramatically.

That day there was an extremely important ceremony which involved an imperial envoy, in the office of the Tokugawa government in the capital Edo. On that day a feudal lord called Asano Takumi no kami Naganori had drawn his sword, which was strictly prohibited in the government offices, and had cut and injured a distinguished top-rank house personnel member called Kira Kozuke no suke. This was a grave incident. As a result of this incident the government ordered the Asano lord to commit seppuku, the Asano clan's position as daimyo was abolished, and all their vassals became ronin. According to the common sense of Bushido, however, if a personal fight breaks out in which both of the parties are to blame, both of the parties have to take responsibility and be judged fairly. But in this incident Kira Kozuke no suke wasn't blamed and escaped punishment.

Forty-seven samurai from the Asano clan, who did not agree with this ruling, vowed to their lord that they would take revenge in his name, and assembled a gang. The next day on December 14th in 1703, they raided the Kira clan and beheaded Kira kozuke no suke, thus redeeming their lord's honor.

At the center of this operation was Horibe Yasube'e. In 1703 he committed seppuku with his fellow warriors and died a glorious death. This incident shows the great power of Nen-ryu kenjutsu and glorifies the ryuha's name. In the long history of Bushido, only he had managed to commit adauchi (revenge) two times in one lifetime, which earned his name a rightful place in the pages of history.

Adauchi is performed only to avenge the murder of one's master, father, brother and so on, and the government only permitted its use to warriors. Farmers, merchants, artisans, and artists were strictly prohibited from carrying it out. If a warrior managed to commit adauchi and kill his opponent, his name and glory as a warrior would be raised, and he would be praised greatly for his deed. Moreover, the side who was the target of the revenge by law could call the other side to a fight and kill him. This was known as "kaeriuchi," and was recognized by society; if the act was successful the counter-avenging side would gain great honor as well. The act of taking revenge became illegal in Japan with the start of the modern period in 1873.

Returning to the Higuchi clan, in the Edo period the 18th successor to the Higuchi clan had developed a technique to deflect flying arrows, and this technique survived until recent years. In recent times, however, the 24th soke, Sadahiro soke, passed away suddenly, and this technique disappeared with him. Therefore, the English channel BBC in 2005, and the German national channel in 2007, stated that in Japan such techniques had been lost. Hearing this story, I decided to open to the public the secret techniques. By doing this, I broke the rules of the ryuha. I made my judgement, however, and merged the Koden Enshin-ryu's hichogiri and the Kuki shin-ryu's yakudaki, and for the first time in public was able to demonstrate cutting an arrow flying at full speed in order to show that the Bushido culture is still prosperous. Moreover, Maniwa nen-ryu is located in Gunma prefecture, and in the dojo there, which was built in 1866, there is an enormous library of ancient books, which are an intangible cultural asset.

When I published a book about Japanese kenjutsu in 1996, Higuchi Sadahiro Soke was extremely kind to help with pictures and guidance, but in the same year his sibling died from illness. Two months later Higuchi Soke himself passed away. Unfortunately, this ryuha currently has stopped its line of Sokes, but these days the husband of Higuchi's only daughter is training, and with the help of the old members, he studies the physical techniques and the mind techniques in order to become the next soke, and continue the legacy.

Master Sadahiro Higuchi, the previous Soke, in Otonashi no kamae.

Yadome no kamae postured by the last Soke Sadahiro Higuchi.

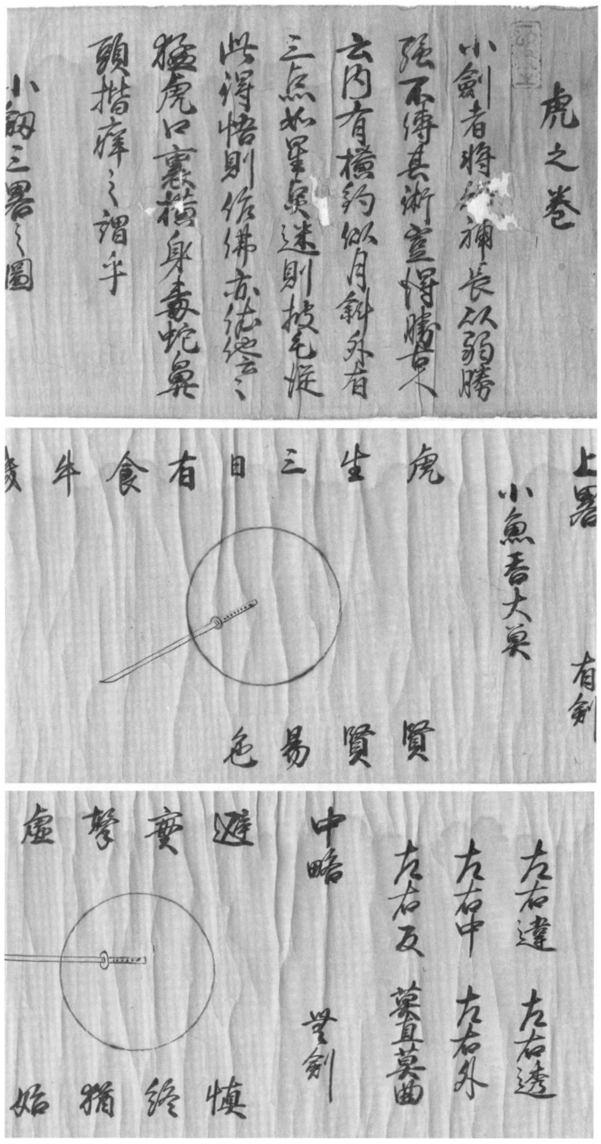

The secret hand scroll of "Tora no maki."

EPILOGUE

Budo, secrets that have been handed down through old books in my family, the Tanaka clan, is the way of the warrior. When the Portuguese missionaries came to Japan around 1500, they reported to their homeland the same thing—Budo is the way of the warrior.

Even these days, the Bushido thought exists subconsciously in the Japanese mind, but the more recently developed styles, such as exercise-oriented kendo, judo, karate, aikido, shorinji kenpo, and modern naginata, among others, are a recreation of the old Budo that is based on new values, such as physical exercise and sportive competition. The centuries-old traditions and thoughts exist only in the traditional ryuhas. Incidentally, the kendo that was born in the Meiji period by the Dainippon Butokukai (Imperial Japan Budo Association) was mixed with some traditional Bushido, but since 1950, when modern kendo emerged, true Bushido all but vanished from kendo.

The founder of judo, Kano Jigoro, wasn't a descendent of a warrior family, he was born to a family of alcohol brewers. As the businessman of those times he had an idea, and by changing the traditional Bushido's jujutsu, he created the sport of judo.

Karate is the tradition of the old people of the Ryukyu islands, which were separate from Japan. In 1879 the Ryukyu islands were forced to annex with Japan, and the name Okinawa was given to them. The Ryukyu people have their own independent culture that stretches over 1,000 years, which includes in it karate; needless to say it has nothing to do with Bushido.

Aikido was founded in the 20th century by Morihei Ueshiba, who was not a descendent of warriors. Ueshiba studied the Daito-ryu, and was devoted to Nakatomi Shinto and the Omotokyo, so aikido was heavily influenced by these new, rising religions.

Shorinji kenpo was founded by Nakano Michiomi, who changed his name to So Doshin. Around 1950, Nakano took the Hakko-ryu jujutsu techniques, and some elements of karate, and mixed them together, founding Shorinji kenpo. Like modern, competitive naginata, it has nothing to do with Bushido.

Original Budo harnesses a constant awareness of danger, and the readiness to die at any moment. One must not forget that others may hold different thoughts and techniques that are at least as great as yours, and be curious about them. Seeking harmony in society and one's surroundings—this way of thinking is the foundation of the ideas of Bushido; from ancient Japan this was the source of aspiration. I want to emphasize that all of the ryuhas that were introduced in this book are genuine, authentic successors of the true Bushido.

Since I started writing this book, one of the things I realized keenly is that the ryuha that have been passed down traditionally from the samurai period until these days all have a glorious history, and each of these ryuha should be written and published as two or three volumes of books. So it is a shame that I couldn't introduce these ryuha sufficiently. Even people who were born after the Meiji Restoration in 1867—the people who have learned techniques from the masters who lived in samurai times and received samurai spirit education—these people who studied the technique and the spirit, and understand it body and soul, still exist.

I also want to emphasize that the sokes and shihans introduced in this book, who studied from masters and became their successors, who inherited the samurai spirit, and who follow the true Budo spirit, are only a few in number. Since 1945, Japan has been influenced for over sixty-five years by America, and even these days the original Japanese culture is disappearing. I think that this will be the last book in which I will introduce the true tradition of Japanese kenjutsu.

In conclusion I would like to thank Ms. Banen Okino and Mr. Ken'ichi Suou, who helped greatly with the collecting and the arranging of the pictures in this book, and to Mr. Hisao Kawakami and Mr. Itamar Zadoff for translation. And last but not least, my deep thanks goes to all the sokes and the shihans of the various ryuhas who showed tremendous kindness in helping me with the material for this book.